The life of Bach

Musical lives

The books in this series each provide an account
of the life of a major composer, considering
both the private and the public figure. The main
thread is biographical and discussion of the
music is integral to the narrative. Each book
thus presents an organic view of the composer,
the music and the circumstances in which the
music was written.

Published titles

21.59

The life of Bach

Peter Williams

CAMBRIDGE
UNIVERSITY PRESS

PUBLISHED BY THE PRESS SYNDICATE OF THE UNIVERSITY OF CAMBRIDGE
The Pitt Building, Trumpington Street, Cambridge, United Kingdom

CAMBRIDGE UNIVERSITY PRESS
The Edinburgh Building, Cambridge, CB2 2RU, UK
40 West 20th Street, New York, NY 10011–4211, USA
477 Williamstown Road, Port Melbourne, VIC 3207, Australia
Ruiz de Alarcón 13, 28014 Madrid, Spain
Dock House, The Waterfront, Cape Town 8001, South Africa

http://www.cambridge.org

First published 2004

Printed in the United Kingdom at the University Press, Cambridge

Typeface FF Quadraat 9.75/14 pt.   System LaTeX 2ε [TB]

A catalogue record for this book is available from the British Library

Library of Congress Cataloguing in Publication data
Williams, Peter F.
The life of Bach / Peter Williams.
        p.   cm. – (Musical lives)
Includes bibliographical references and index.
ISBN 0–521–82636–5
1. Bach, Johann Sebastian, 1685–1750. 2. Composers – Germany – Biography.
I. Title. II. Series.
ML410.B1W71   2003   780′.92–dc21   2003055080
[B]

ISBN 0 521 82636 5 hardback
ISBN 0 521 53374 0 paperback

CONTENTS

ILLUSTRATIONS

ACKNOWLEDGMENTS

I would like to thank Penny Souster of Cambridge University Press for proposing and encouraging this book; Michael Black and Laura Davey for improvements to it; Prof. Dr Hans Joachim Schulze, Dr Andreas Glöckner and Dr Dana Albertus of Leipzig, Dr John E. Druesedow Jr of Duke University, North Carolina, and Gill Jones of Cardiff University for kind help; the Irving S. Gilmore Music Library, Yale University (photographs from the *Clavierbüchlein* of W. F. Bach); William H. Scheide (photograph of 1748 Haussmann portrait); the National Gallery of Ireland (photograph of the painting of Dresden by Bernardo Bellotto); the Stadtgeschichtliches Museum, Altes Rathaus, Leipzig (photograph of the Gebhardt sword); and the Stadt- und Bergbaumuseum, Freiberg, Saxony (photograph of the engraving of the Freiberg cantata performance). Other illustrations are from the author's own collection.

Introduction

The biggest problem in writing about J. S. Bach is that so little is known about either his inner or his outer life, less than for any great composer since his time. So his admirers (as seems also to be the case with Shakespeare) find it hard to avoid inferring what they can from context and from a large number of extant and incomparable works. The second problem is that the few known facts, and even the relevant illustrations, are constantly regurgitated, leaving readers with the same few details over and over again. Or they are reinterpreted in the light of an author's own preoccupations, which might well not be the composer's. The third problem is that he was a largely untravelled eighteenth-century German Lutheran, thus remote on several counts from today's English readers, who can do no more than press their faces to the window and look in.

There is a further difficulty: the exquisite world of imagination opened up by any powerful music is itself problematic, for it tempts listeners to put into words the feelings it arouses in them and so to visualise a composer's priorities and even personality. There must be few people who have played, sung, listened to or written about Bach's music who do not feel they have a special understanding of him, a private connection, unique to themselves, but ultimately coming from their idea of what music is and does. This might be quite different from the composer's. And yet, if only because of the sparse biographical details, a life of Bach must pay especially close attention to his music, and I have therefore referred to the works themselves more often than authors of some other books in this series have done. This is partly to fill in the chronology, partly to imply what his interests were at particular moments.

Because of the sparse documentation, authors of Bach biographies have often chosen to earmark their book with a subtitle, 'Bach the musician-poet' or 'Bach the culmination of an era' or 'Bach the learned musician', interpreting the life and works accordingly. But any such subtitle is likely to be both unremittingly reverential and inclined to anachronism. Perhaps a realistic approach to his occasional weaknesses can be quite as instructive, particularly when one points to music in which art seems to take second place to artifice. Bach biographers could usefully probe these weaknesses more than they usually do, not least because their subject may have had his own ideas on what constitutes 'weakness'.

One thread leading through the maze of masterworks is supplied by the so-called Bach Obituary, written probably within six months of his death but published only in 1754, a delay not uncommon in Germany at the time and not necessarily implying faint public interest. Like any biography, the Obituary had an agenda of its own, relaying what its period and its university-educated authors, C. P. E. Bach and J. F. Agricola, found important to say about a period and a man they understood only in part. In doing this they laid a path which admirers have trodden ever since. Consequently, what they say and do not say can be taken as a starting point, something to relate to other evidence and to use for shaping a short biography such as this one.

Much as John Mainwaring was soon to do for Handel, the Bach Obituary makes some attempt to list not only biographical details but some of the composer's personal characteristics, and since the Obituary authors can have known him intimately only during the Leipzig years, I have listed what they say of this sort in the last chapter. Though brief, their remarks about the composer imply more than might appear. For example, by referring more than once to his sense of obligation 'to God and to his neighbour' they reaffirm Lutheran orthodoxy's two-fold duty, unfamiliar now that the idea of piety has deteriorated, but once fundamental. Compared to such ideas, today's searches in Bach's music for number symbolism, rhetoric, Golden Sections, biblical hermeneutics, cosmological allusion, even political agendas and psychological states may be satisfying only the ephemeral interests of our own time.

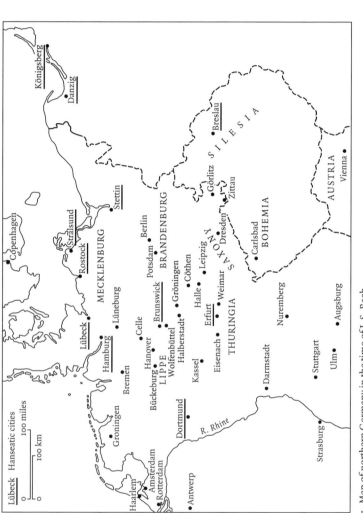

1 Map of northern Germany in the time of J. S. Bach.

1 Early years, 1685–1703

Johann Sebastian Bach belongs [sic] to a family in all of whose
members equally a love for and skill in music seem, as a
common gift, to have been imparted by nature.

The Obituary's chief author, C. P. E. Bach (Emanuel), was well aware
of the musical part of his family's history as it had been handed down,
for although his father seems to have contributed little if anything to
the day's published biographies, he spent time compiling a genealogical table, the 'Origin of the musical-Bach family' ('Ursprung
der musicalisch-Bachischen Familie', Dok I, pp. 255–67). He did this
at or around the age of fifty, and Emanuel added to it. It numbers fifty-
three Bachs over some two hundred years, many of them professional
musicians well known in central Germany, though only one or two became so in a larger Europe – himself and, as perhaps he could anticipate
by 1735, some of his sons.

One can imagine the personal reasons why a composer would compile such a table at or near his half century, especially after suffering
so many bereavements from early childhood on: his parents (mother
at fifty, father two days short of fifty), gradually all seven of his siblings
(he was the youngest), a wife, no fewer than ten children and a beloved
employer. The wider the extended Bach family in Thuringia, the more
constantly news of deaths circulated. In addition, J. S. Bach might have

been open as much to the day's fashions as to any atavistic compulsions of his own. For genealogies were well known in the book centre of Leipzig, where, throughout the 1720s and 1730s, Johann Hübner was publishing aristocratic and other family tables for what was evidently a ready market. One such book had some 333 tables.

In its pride at the size and musical achievements of the large clan to which he, a child-orphan, belonged, Bach's table is doing two things: establishing the story of an exceptional family and saluting an art practised to the greater glory of God. The story is not a fairy tale but sets out an (as it were) apostolic succession, not entirely unlike the genealogical tables in two Gospels and parts of the Pentateuch, consciously or otherwise. Chiefly as a result of it, the Bachs have become the best-known musical family, though positions of higher prestige were occupied by some of the Couperin family in Paris. The first name in the table, Veit Bach, was that of a man said to have fled Hungary for his Lutheran faith, and although this is doubtful – Hungary (meaning modern Slovakia?) had early on become predominantly Protestant – from Veit a Tree of Jesse springs, a genealogy of Protestant church musicians active over generations.

Probably a few years later, the table was joined by another family document, the Old-Bach Archive, a collection of choral works by older family members, inluding Sebastian's father and first father-in-law. The collection seems to have passed to J. S. Bach on the death (and perhaps by particular request) of his first cousin Johann Ernst in 1739, an organist who like Sebastian had studied in Hamburg, and who succeeded him at Arnstadt in 1708. Both the Archive and the main copy of the table passed later to Emanuel Bach.

By the 1730s, music as an honourable family trade reflected the growing respect for art and the artist, 'Kunst, der Künstler': this was not a dynasty of shoemakers. A surgeon and a shopkeeper who qualified for listing among the table's 'musical Bachs' were, one can assume, gifted amateurs, unlike the Bach who had been a court jester but is not included, despite Sebastian's certain knowledge of him (Geiringer 1954, p. 9). Of course, the list also excludes the mothers, wives and daughters. In a letter of 1748, Bach informs a cousin of Emanuel's 'two male heirs' without mentioning their sister, for it was the boys through whom the family tree grew further. Yet his own mother, a Lämmerhirt, was undoubtedly musical, being a member of a family closely connected with music in Erfurt, the region's largest city. She was related to other significant musicians, composers to whose music J. S. Bach was to respond in one way or another: J. G. Walther (as stepsister to his great-aunt) and J. H. Buttstedt (as second cousin to his wife). (See below for remarks on Bach's engagement with the music of 'minor composers'.) Something surely came to Sebastian from his mother, as it came to his sons from their mothers, both of whose original families were also musical.

It would be something to wonder at that such fine men should be so little known outside their fatherland, if one did not consider that these honourable Thuringians were so content with their fatherland and their status that they would not venture far from it, even to go after their fortune.

Sons of Bach would assume that normally success could only be measured by going away to study or by occupying a position of prestige away from home, in a royal court of renown, such as Emanuel's in Potsdam at the time of the Obituary. For some decades the garrulous Hamburg critic Johann Mattheson had been lionising Handel and reporting on his successes in England, and news of Handel's great if fluctuating wealth had reached his native city of Halle nearby. Bach's successor at Leipzig, Gottlob Harrer, had 'spent some time in Italy' (Dok II, p. 480), as Emanuel, who also applied for the job, admitted he had not (Dok III, p. 255). Telemann, Emanuel's godfather, had travelled, come into contact with Polish music, written operas for the free city of Hamburg, visited Paris and actually declined the Leipzig cantorate: a varied and productive musical life of fame and patent success. At about the time the Obituary was published, Emanuel's younger brother Johann Christian was leaving to study in Italy, perhaps with the renowned Padre

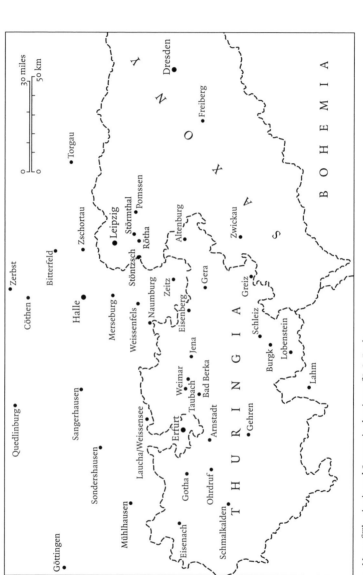

2 Map of Thuringia and Saxony in the time of J. S. Bach.

Martini, and soon found success in Milan and London, freelancing in the modern way.

How far the Obituary is reporting Bach's own views can only be guessed: the various grumbles he expressed over pay and conditions, particularly in Leipzig in his forties and fifties, and no doubt aloud *en famille*, may have led to a search for some form of self-justification. The Obituary authors, too, though better travelled, needed to claim the self-sufficiency of provincial learning. One hopes that for Bach there was genuine 'contentment with his fatherland': it would be dreadful to imagine him towards the end of his life regretting how he had spent it, wondering what he had missed in the musical centres of Europe, and having to find consolation by willing himself to be content with what he had done 'for God and his neighbour'.

Contentment of this kind had already been implied in biographies of German heroes familiar to Bach and his sons, such as Camerarius's life of Melanchthon, the early reformer and revered colleague of Luther. Melanchthon too was orphaned (aged eleven), expressed fidelity to his fatherland and place of origin, was headstrong, and educated himself by assiduously studying what others had written: all motifs to occur in the Bach Obituary. By 1700, several editions of Melanchthon's *Life* had been published in Leipzig, and his directives on preaching and scriptural exegesis were especially influential. (Melanchthon was drawn by Albrecht Dürer, who, though well travelled, similarly let it be known that he preferred remaining in Nuremberg to seeking fame and riches elsewhere. His family was also said to have originated in Hungary.) To knowledgable listeners for whom a cantata was 'musical rhetoric' equivalent to the verbal rhetoric of a sermon as laid out by Melanchthon, parallels between the reformer and J. S. Bach would have appeared close.

To see Thuringia as a geographical crossroads where 'the manifold European trends met and merged' (Wolff 2000, p. 16) is rather wishful thinking. Travel overland being as difficult as it was, really lively contact between distant cities on major water routes such as Amsterdam–London or Dresden–Hamburg would have been no harder than between

Dresden and Eisenach. But a narrow province with lively traditions does have advantages: self-contained Thuringia was a province with a strong culture, concentrated on itself, competitive and vigorous in its artistic endeavours. (Compare Shakespeare's London.) Here, an exceptionally gifted and voracious boy would be stimulated to learn what he could from elsewhere and to rely on his own achievements. Of course, local or national pride can mean underrating the foreign, as shown by the Obituary's sarcastic references to Louis Marchand later. Nevertheless, it is – to this day – more typical of Protestant than of Roman Catholic cultures to be receptive to foreign achievement or to seek personal development abroad, and provincial Thuringia was no exception.

The Obituary's word 'fortune' denotes both financial and artistic success. Certainly Bach did progress financially over his career, doing so without the kind of risks Handel took. Reckoned in terms of annual income in guilders, as a young court musician Bach earned 28, as a minor parish organist 50 then 85, as court organist 150 then 200, as concertmeister 250 to 300, as court capellmeister 450 and as cantor about 800, in addition to not insignificant payment in kind at each stage (fuel, cereals, lodging, etc.). But clearly, his fame and fortune did not match Handel's.

Johann Sebastian Bach was born in 1685, on 21 March, in Eisenach. His parents were Johann Ambrosius Bach, court and town musician there, and Elisabeth (née Lämmerhirt), daughter of a town official in Erfurt.

Only after describing the composer's context in general terms does the Obituary turn to its main subject, but from those two brief sentences readers would learn much about his background. Some idea of the significance of Eisenach – a city associated with Tannhäuser, a medieval minstrels' combat, a saint (Elizabeth of Thuringia), Martin Luther (a native, translating the New Testament imprisoned in its castle) and J. S. Bach (who latinised its name in some of his signatures) – may be gained by imagining Stratford-on-Avon as not only the birthplace of Shakespeare but the site of Richard Lionheart's pilgrimage, the mission of St Boniface, a famous bardic contest, and a prison in which Milton wrote *Paradise Lost*. Careful readers of Walther's *Lexicon* of 1732 would also have known that 21 March was less than four weeks after the birth of Georg Frideric Handel in Halle, a bigger town beyond Thuringia and by 1732 the proud seat of a university.

While Johann was a common family name, 'Sebastian' came from the godfather, as was customary: Sebastian Nagel, *Stadtpfeifer* or municipal musician in Eisenach and a colleague of Ambrosius. By the time of Sebastian's birth Ambrosius had served as director of the town's music for fourteen years, having previously been a municipal violinist in Erfurt, where he had married Elisabeth Lämmerhirt, daughter of a town councillor and thus bourgeois by class. Had Ambrosius succeeded a few months earlier in obtaining the release he sought from his Eisenach position and returned to Erfurt, Sebastian would have been born there, as his brother Christoph had been, the brother who was to take him in later. It was also to Erfurt relatives that his sister Marie Salome returned when their mother died.

Erfurt plays a big part in Sebastian's musical background. Its musicians over the years included Pachelbel (who taught Christoph from 1686), Nicolaus Vetter and Buttstedt (Pachelbel pupils), Johann Effler (Sebastian's predecessor in Weimar), Walther (a Buttstedt pupil) and Jacob Adlung (organist and influential writer on organs). Various Bachs remained prominent town musicians there right until Napoleonic times. In 1716 Sebastian returned to test a new organ in the Augustinerkirche, Erfurt's 'Austin Friars', where Luther himself was ordained priest in 1507. This organ was the work of the privileged Erfurt builder J. G. Schröter, with whose family Sebastian remained in contact, and whose pupils included Franciscus Volckland, builder of several instruments around Erfurt still in recognisable condition today.

Judging by his position, Bach's father was a gifted musician, officially praised as a versatile and effective music director (BJ 1927, p. 141), much better paid than his predecessor in Eisenach, and presumably a good violinist. His duties at Eisenach included playing wind music twice a day from a balcony or tower of the town hall, participating in the music in St George's church (the church of Sebastian's baptism) on Sundays and feast days (main service and vespers), and in various ceremonial events, civic or private, for which he had the *privilegium*. Whether such musicians as Ambrosius considered themselves primarily wind or string players is not obvious, but to judge by the support shown to his eventual widow by the cantor of St George's, his senior colleague, he and his family were respected (*Dok* II, p. 4).

Although cantor A. C. Dedekind would have been known to young Sebastian, a more certain influence on him was the church's organist at the time, Ambrosius's cousin and colleague, another Johann Christoph Bach. In his genealogical table, Sebastian uniquely calls this Bach 'a profound composer', one of whose motets he probably planned for his own funeral. It is often conjectured now that as an active organist and composer – neither of which Ambrosius is known to have been – Christoph allowed the boy to learn as many basics of organ playing and construction as were feasible, though had he been a formal teacher, the table would have said so. Christoph laboured many years to improve the large organ in what was the town's major church, St George's, and perhaps the boy was as much interested in this as he was in accompanying his father to his various duties. Musicians had close contacts, and presumably Ambrosius's sons sang in St George's choir, whose repertory included some music by Josquin, a composer admired in writing by Luther himself.

Sebastian's schooling is uncertain before 1693 when he entered the Latin school in which Luther had been a pupil two hundred years earlier and which taught German and Latin literacy, confessional study such as the catechism and psalms, and presumably some degree of numeracy. That he was younger at entry than his brothers, went straight into the fifth rather than sixth (a lower) class and by 1695 was placed higher than his elder brother Jacob suggests he was a brighter than average child.

Johann Sebastian was still not ten years old when he found himself deprived of his parents by death. He made his way to Ohrdruf to his eldest brother, Johann Christoph (organist there), under whose guidance he laid the foundations for his keyboard playing.

Whether any pathos was intended in the Obituary's words 'still not ten years old' or 'made his way', and if so whether it came from the composer himself, cannot be certain. Both add a shade of meaning beyond the brute facts, and perhaps Emanuel did not know that another orphaned brother, Jacob, also went to Ohrdruf. Certainly neither boy's prospect can have been good at that moment.

Also unknown is whether the younger orphan's loss affected him in such a way as to lead to the single-mindedness, defiance and even irascibility that people have read into the pitifully small number of later documents concerning him. Handel lost his father around his twelfth birthday, but his biographer notes only that it 'produced a considerable change for the worse in the income of his mother' (Mainwaring 1760, p. 29), a remark probably from Handel himself: again, it is not personal feelings but practical circumstances – could the boy now afford further training in music, etc. – that are the business of biography. Bach's mother had died before his father, about 1 May 1694, so there was less of a financial problem at that point. Sebastian and Jacob had then remained with their father, who remarried some seven months later, only to die barely three months after that, leaving a wife who already had children of her own.

So common was bereavement and so normal for relations to take in orphans – Sebastian's parents had too, and Emanuel was to take in his brother Johann Christian – that one can only guess how the deaths were taken, how much financial anxiety there was when Christoph became responsible for two younger brothers, and how problematic life became in any regard for any of them. Christoph himself was only twenty-three at the time, married a year before. His younger brothers received charity income (free board) as poor scholars, Sebastian for a longer period as a chorister. Whether what the Obituary calls his foundations as a keyboardist were laid by Christoph in regular lessons or as circumstances allowed is not recorded, though it may be wrong to assume that young musicians merely picked up what they could within an active musical family. There would have been music copying to do, spinets to tune, services to deputise in.

From age fourteen, and presumably at his father's cost, Christoph had studied three years with Pachelbel in Erfurt and – to judge by his impressive MSS of organ music – become a player with wide interests, indeed an 'artistic man', 'optimus artifex', according to church registers. Perhaps he had picked up an interest in French organ music from Pachelbel and passed it on to his younger brother. His recent marriage had been the occasion for some music in which their father had participated with Pachelbel himself, whom presumably the boy Sebastian saw on that occasion. Ohrdruf was a minor town in comparison with Eisenach, but St Michael's church library was better than many, and the organ was meant to be adequate for all the repertory of the time. According to the contract of 1690 (BJ 1926, pp. 145ff.), it was to have two manuals and twenty-one stops, including chair organ and a pedal solo stop for chorales with cantus firmus. Construction work on it in the late 1690s could well have interested a young teenager.

Walther's Lexicon of 1732 says that Sebastian learnt 'the first principles' of keyboard playing from his brother, and according to Emanuel 'nothing more than that' (Dok III, p. 288) – that is to say, the boy taught himself composition. In broad terms both statements might be true, but the second was also part of a picture of self-reliance consistently drawn by Emanuel, who was adjusting for later readers what was said in Walther's book. (So little did Emanuel know of his father's Ohrdruf period that he thought Christoph died in 1700 and left the fifteen-year-old to make his own way: see below.) Both brothers had a lively interest in both local and 'foreign' keyboard music. Had his father still been alive, Sebastian would presumably have worked just as much on string instruments, but as it was he was soon producing imitations of the various kinds of keyboard music composed by the accepted masters of the region, Pachelbel and Kuhnau. Some organ chorales attributed to J. S. Bach probably date from about this time, his mid-teens, including some of the so-called Neumeister collection, BWV 1090–1120, chorales not always distinguishable from the work of Pachelbel pupils. In some of these modest pieces, however, there is both a sureness of harmonic touch and an imaginative waywardness in the treatment that one would dearly like to be proved authentic.

It is odd that there is still some uncertainty as to who composed what amongst these and other keyboard pieces, but 1700 was too soon for conspicuously gifted boys to be such a wonder that their work would be systematically preserved. As a recognised phenomenon, the child prodigy barely existed yet in music, particularly in composition. Fortunately, the Ohrdruf Lyceum registers at least show Sebastian to have been successful in school, being fourth in the *prima* class (largely for eighteen-year-olds, and with a wide curriculum) when he left in March 1700. Another sign that he was smarter than most?

A book full of keyboard pieces by the then most famous masters Froberger, Kerll and Pachelbel, which his brother owned, was however denied him. [Nevertheless, he] copied it by moonlight. After six months this musical booty was happily in his own hands, [and he] was attempting to put it to use when, to his greatest dismay, his brother became aware of it and mercilessly took from him the copy he had prepared with such trouble.

This must have been a large book, to take six months to copy (even in secret) and to provoke such a reaction. Considering how few intimate details there are in the Obituary, this episode must have loomed large in family tradition, and touches on motifs familiar in any musician's life.

Several things can be learnt from it, therefore. The MS was of keyboard music and contained work by 'southern' composers (Froberger and Kerll were Roman Catholic, Pachelbel was by now working in Nuremberg); it gives a glimpse of how a young musician *in statu pupillari* learnt by copying music, as does another MS from this period but associated with the young Handel;[1] and it gives a picture of how industrious and single-minded the young Bach was, how deep his feelings were, how much he deserves our sympathy. Another evocative and verisimilar detail is that the MS could be rolled up and pulled through the grill-doors of the cupboard by little fingers, though quite how this was done is not easy to envisage. This and the 'six months' could be nestorian embellishment.

The original narrator of the story, whether Emanuel or his father, meant to give a sense of the boy's several virtues, but how far either had meant to malign the elder brother is uncertain. Since Christoph himself seems to have been content to remain an organist, one could read either personal envy or genuine solicitude in the anecdote. Either way, unauthorised copying of valuable and hard-won professional materials was improper, especially if they were then put to use, as the Obituary says they were. (Was the boy presuming to play them in his brother's church?) Equally improper was defiance of a guardian in loco parentis, one solicitous, amongst other things, for a younger brother's eyesight.

Perhaps there was a further, more musical reason for Christoph's action: their father had been a violinist active in various musical spheres, and Sebastian, if brought up properly, could look ahead to being more than a church organist. If he developed as a string player, as could have been his father's wish, he might become capellmeister to a great king or, better still, opera and music director of an important city. Too single-minded a pursuit of keyboard music would lead at best only to the cantorate of a major church . . .

At what point the young Bach dedicated his Capriccio in E major BWV 993 to his brother is not known, though its turgid formlessness and harmonic poverty are early signs. This piece suggests at least two things, one musical, one personal: that already the young composer was interested in creating length, in sustaining a movement without the aid of a text or programme; and that despite the moonlight episode there was a positive contact between the brothers. This last is also

[1] Lost but documented, containing music by Zachow, Alberti, Froberger, Krieger, Kerll, Strungk and others: see HHB, p. 17.

suggested by Christoph's extant books of music – the richly comprehensive Andreas Bach Book and Möller MS – to which Sebastian probably contributed some of his own and other composers' music. On the personal level, some years later, in 1708, Christoph's wife was godmother to Sebastian's first child, as in 1713 Sebastian was godfather to one of Christoph's twin sons. Another of his sons, Bernhard, came to Weimar in 1715 to study with his uncle, going on to an appointment at Cöthen in 1719, no doubt also on his recommendation (*Dok* II, pp. 47, 202–3). As to the moonlight episode, the Obituary says that Bach had the book returned to him only on his brother's death. This could have been via Bernhard, but if Emanuel and his father were unsure when Christoph died, perhaps the book had been returned long before and subsequently lost.

The motif of adult resistance to a child's musical gifts is found again in Mainwaring's biography of Handel, who, when his father

> forbad him to meddle with any musical instrument . . . found means to get a little clavichord privately convey'd to a room at the top of the house. To this room he constantly stole when the family was asleep
> (Mainwaring 1760, p. 5)

and presumably he played by moonlight. Mainwaring also refers to the mathematician Pascal, a child prodigy who pursued studies 'against the consent of [his] parents, and in spite of all the opposition'. So an exceptionally gifted child conquers resistance and is noted for his persistence. Furthermore, studying by moonlight was itself a desirable motif for an orphan's biography: it appears again in Melanchthon's, and suggests an ardent young spirit, self-reliant, never afraid of hard work and of self-improving study.

> [In 1700] Johann Sebastian made his way, in company with one of his schoolfellows, called Erdmann . . . to Lüneburg and St Michael's Gymnasium there, [where] our Bach, because of his unusually fine soprano voice, was well received.

The Obituary claimed that the move occurred on Christoph's death, but this was not for another twenty-one years. Whether Bach had forgotten or was suing for sympathy (the lone orphan) or whether Emanuel had misunderstood and/or was guessing is not known, although the genealogical table had also left Christoph's dates blank (Dok I, p. 259).

Fifteen was an age when generally boys became more independent, as apprentices: at about that age Christoph himself had gone to Pachelbel, and at fourteen Jacob had gone back to Eisenach as apprentice to his father's successor. Rather than remain locally, Sebastian sang well enough to take himself off to an important establishment farther north, surely a sign of higher horizons. To be 'well received' there, if it actually happened, meant recognition for the boy's gifts; if it was only a later claim, it was an important one to make, comparable to the praise given to the maturer Bach by the doyen of north German church musicians, Adam Reinken.

As an orphan Bach had qualified for charity money, though not beyond the watershed fifteenth birthday. It could have been his brother's cantor Elias Herda who arranged for Bach and his friend to go to the fine northern city of Lüneburg, to sing in St Michael's and attend school there (Dok I, p. 69), in time for Easter 1700 – a week before he was fifteen and perhaps only a few weeks before his 'uncommonly beautiful treble' voice broke, in the words of Emanuel, who either assumed this or had it from his father (Dok III, p. 82). Voices often broke later than nowadays, and it was not unknown for fifteen-year-olds to continue in a choir school. Erdmann was three years older and by then a *Bassist*; but it is not impossible that Sebastian's voice settled so quickly that he too could soon sing both bass and countertenor. He remained a scholar in the top class (the *prima*) until 1702, in a school known to have had a distinguished curriculum, including rhetoric, Greek, and German verse, and where the church library was also unusually well stocked.

Although the move to Lüneburg is unlikely to have gone against the fifteen-year-old's wishes, whether he had a conscious desire to study organs and organ playing in north Germany is uncertain, even if he did admire the music. Perhaps a recent book, Werckmeister's *Orgelprobe*, which he certainly knew at some point (see below, p. 41), had whetted his appetite for hearing big instruments with colourful effects, including those built in Hamburg by the unrivalled Arp Schnitger, who wrote a dedicatory poem for Werckmeister's book. Or perhaps he had an inkling that his voice was about to break, and took steps to be in a distinguished church choir in a cosmopolitan city when it happened, one where he might hope to find a suitable apprenticeship.

It is striking that, unlike his brother, Sebastian did not go off to study with Pachelbel, who was by then a respected teacher in Nuremberg, a city of some importance and closer to Ohrdruf than Lüneburg. Closer still were Halle, where the famed Zachow had taught the young Handel in 1698 (HHB, p. 17), and Leipzig, where Kuhnau was admired and not yet vexed by the pushy Telemann. Was the reason for going to Lüneburg personal – he was really close friends with Georg Erdmann? Or, more significantly, cultural – the Lutheranism of Nuremberg or Halle was too Low Church for him? Or, most likely, partly musical, partly personal – in Lüneburg there worked Georg Böhm, whose music would surely have impressed him more than would Pachelbel's, Zachow's, Kuhnau's or Reinken's, and who had links with the young Bach through family connections in Ohrdruf, his own birthplace? There is something in the make-up of J. S. Bach that allows one to think he could both explore family connections and at the same time follow where a discriminating or ambitious taste led him.

> From Lüneburg he travelled from time to time to Hamburg, to hear the then famous organist of St Catherine's, Johann Adam Reinken.

Further questions arise here too. Was one reason for the Lüneburg move to study further with a northern master, to seek an apprenticeship in Hamburg which, because Bach had no money for one, did not materialise? Did he really go there several times, as the Obituary said? Did he seek Reinken in Hamburg rather than the more gifted Buxtehude in Lübeck because in Ohrdruf Reinken's music had been better known, being published? Or because Hamburg was nearer than Lübeck? Or was it that for musicians of Emanuel Bach's generation Reinken's longevity made him better known than Buxtehude, and that, for the purposes of an Obituary, his fame bestowed more credit on the young Bach? Another possibility is that Hamburg attracted him for a reason not recognised by the Obituary authors – for its opera, by now in the hands of Reinhard Keiser, whose directorship later drew the young Handel to Hamburg. Bach's eventual first job as a court musician (see below) might mean that he had looked earlier in the direction of courts and theatres.

These are some of the possible questions which, were one to know the answers, could give some idea of the kind of boy the young Bach was – whether he planned his career carefully, whether he made decisions for professional or personal reasons, whether he was at the time as interested exclusively in keyboard and church music as the Obituary wished to suggest. It could be that he did later recognise Buxtehude as the more important master, hence taking leave from his job in 1705 for the express purpose of studying with him (see below). But either way, simply to 'hear Reinken' cannot be the whole story: for a young man to study with such established church musicians, outside the auspices of a school or university, the most promising arrangement would have been to take up some kind of apprenticeship with one or other of them. Could the young Bach not afford this?

Curiously, at this point the Obituary does not mention Georg Böhm, whose church of St John was the biggest in Lüneburg, and who may have recommended the boy go to Hamburg, again for the purpose of putting a foot on the career ladder. Böhm is not known to have been directly connected to the Michaeliskirche or its choir but was nevertheless the most gifted, inspiring organ composer Sebastian could have heard so far, with an unusual melodic flair for setting chorales and a sense of drama in other works. In his *Lexicon* of 1732, Walther again gives much more space to Reinken than to Böhm, and this could have influenced the Obituary writers. In a later letter, Emanuel actually crossed out the phrase 'his Lüneburg teacher Böhm' to replace it with 'the Lüneburg organist Böhm' (Dok III, p. 290), but this conforms to the old image of the self-taught composer, learning (like Melanchthon) *sine duce*, without a guide. Quite possibly the fifteen-year-old had hoped to become Böhm's assistant, then turned to the northern masters. But many of Bach's earlier organ works, such as the praeludia in C major and D minor, are closer to Böhm's style than to anyone else's, unaware of this though Emanuel very likely was. And the two composers were still in contact in 1727, as is clear from Böhm having copies of two of Bach's harpsichord partitas for sale.

'To hear Reinken' is thus part of the self-taught picture: Bach neither took lessons as such nor became an apprentice-assistant but made study visits, to a major figure in a major church of a major Hanseatic city. Though not as old as was later thought, Reinken was nevertheless a venerable musician who presided at the famous organ of the Katharinenkirche, and was known to look after it exceptionally well. The instrument had some sixty stops including 32′ reed, distributed over four manuals in the style of Arp Schnitger, the Hamburg builder. J. F. Agricola, a later pupil of Bach and part-author of the Obituary, said that Bach admired not only this great Hamburg organ but the fine condition in which Reinken kept it (*Dok* III, p. 191). In other words, Reinken was a master such as the Obituary envisaged and admired: both artistic and practical, both a creative musician and a skilled player *au fait* with his instrument's technicalities. But Böhm also had an unusually fine organ in the Johanniskirche, Lüneburg, and it would be strange if he were not a similarly careful curator of it.

Hamburg's varied musical life in theatre and church was well known to Böhm, even though the Obituary does not draw attention to it: its preference was to establish Bach's credentials as organist, much as Walther's *Lexicon* did when it told of another significant German organist, Georg Leyding, visiting Reinken for the same purpose. Did these young musicians really have no interest in Hamburg's music outside the church? That is hard to believe, and certainly, in more ways than one, Hamburg composers left their mark on Bach, for at some point he arranged chamber sonatas by Reinken for keyboard (e.g. BWV 965 and 966, perhaps as late as 1715), copied F. N. Brauns's *St Mark Passion* (performing it in Weimar, as later in Leipzig?) and came to compose arias of a kind made familiar by Hamburg opera composers, either to Bach direct or to others (such as Telemann) who impinged on him.

Like so many organs with which Bach came into contact, in Eisenach, Ohrdruf, Weimar and Leipzig, the instrument in the Lüneburg Michaeliskirche was regularly being worked on. Its mishmash of historical periods – a big Gothic main organ with pedal pulldowns, Baroque chair organ and a *Brustwerk* – made it desirable for the organist to keep to old genres such as stereophonic toccatas, simple chorale settings and variations based on common-property formulas. Other musical experiences would be necessary before Bach could develop his music in newer directions.

> And from here too he had the chance, through frequent listening to a then famous band kept by the Duke of Celle (consisting largely of Frenchmen), to give himself a good grounding in French taste, which at the time was something quite new in those parts.

Once again, the Obituary says nothing about the young Bach having teachers but shows him learning 'through frequent listening' to various kinds of music. So having as a boy sung the standard repertory in one important Lutheran parish church, then heard Reinken play and direct in another, now he was experiencing French music as performed by French instrumentalists in a duke's *cappella*. Handel's biography, too, at a similar point in his life, finds it important to testify to its subject's grasp not only of local German church music but also of French and in his case Italian styles, claiming amongst other things that he had instructed Corelli himself 'in the manner of executing these spirited passages' in French *ouvertures* (Mainwaring 1760, p. 56).

The Duke of Lüneburg-Celle's band played in Lüneburg,[2] and since, as the Obituary uncharacteristically points out, the players themselves were mostly Frenchmen (thanks to the duke's Huguenot wife?), the

---

[2] The Obituary's phrase 'from here' ('von Lüneburg aus') suggests that the authors thought Bach had to go to Celle to hear the band.

composer could have spoken of the experience so as to give an impression that he had learnt about French styles from the horse's mouth. One would indeed learn more from French players than from the way the music was notated, for this gives only a pale impression of how vivid and tuneful the apparently convention-choked music of France actually is. A good string group would have introduced the young Bach to rhetorical gesture and such expressive articulation as he is unlikely to have heard either from local musicians or in the average Lutheran cantata. Parisian wind players would have given ideas on what a minuet or bourrée or gavotte was better than any German harpsichord suite. The full ensemble, if good enough, produced harmony of a sensuousness out of place in church, and the manner of playing it – the rhythms, rubato, articulation, ornaments – would, one imagines, have been a revelation to any imaginative young musician.

A clear grasp of French style is evident throughout Bach's creative life, from the early keyboard overture in F major BWV 820 right through to a movement in the Art of Fugue, BWV 1080.vi. Others such as Telemann must have learnt from similar experiences, and certainly Handel had done so already by the time of his first operas in Hamburg (1705). One can assume that Bach heard *ouvertures* or ballet suites played by the Celle band, something entirely different from Reinken's organ music, if not from Böhm's. Perhaps Böhm was responsible for suggesting these visits to the duke's band, having himself previously learnt something of French *manière* from the Hamburg opera director J. S. Kusser, who had studied with Lully. Handel too had learnt enough in Hamburg about ballet suites to preface his first opera in Italy, *Rodrigo* (1707), with a fine, extensive and idiomatic example. The Duke of Celle's theatre had Italian opera for a time, but it was the French court ensemble founded in 1666 that became famous.

Many details in the F major suite BWV 820 signal the young Bach's keen ear, with harmonic, rhythmic and melodic details typical – too thoroughly typical, even – of a Parisian composer of c1690. For example, it imitates the way French string players ended the stately dotted-note first section of an *ouverture* with a big chord the first time but not on the repeat, when the first violin shoots off with a lively fugue – a subtle detail that takes the word 'fuga' ('flight') literally. To what extent his visits first introduced Bach to typical French harmonies, rich discords, characteristic bowings, leaning grace notes and lilting rhythms is hard to know, since church music would not have been the place for them. But he certainly maintained an interest in French keyboard music, and it is probably fair to say that his overtures for orchestra (BWV 1066–1069) and later for harpsichord (especially in C minor, BWV 831a) enrich the original elegant French style with a carefulness, harmonic sophistication, melody and counterpoint seldom if ever found in France itself.

2 First appointments, 1703–1708

In 1703 he went to Weimar, and became a musician of the court there.

It seems that Bach completed two years at the Lüneburg school, visited Hamburg either during them or subsequently, then returned to Thuringia (to his brother?), applied to become organist at Sangerhausen in July 1702, and went into service at Weimar in January 1703. This order of events, which is not quite certain, would be rather the reverse of Handel's, who briefly became organist at home in Halle in 1702 and then travelled to Hamburg, launched on his many-sided career. But when Handel's biographer says that, not wishing to add to his widowed mother's expenses, 'the first thing which he did . . . was to procure scholars, and obtain some employment in the orchestra' (Mainwaring 1760, p. 29), he is describing a situation not entirely different from that of the seventeen-year-old Bach in Weimar.

Why Bach returned to Thuringia and left the wider musical promise of Lüneburg and Hamburg can only be guessed: disappointment (no job offers), personal preferences, a wish to succeed his father's cousin Christoph in Eisenach? Doubtless he needed income and by then may have learnt that he preferred the world of church and court music to that of opera and city theatres, in which case the return says much about him. But one cannot know this for certain, nor even whether he knew of the Sangerhausen vacancy from contacts he had maintained at home or had merely heard about it en route from Lüneburg to Thuringia. (Sangerhausen could have been on the way home.) Whichever is the case, it seems he had enough skill and a good enough CV to be successful with his application.

In such a society, a seventeen-year-old is not likely to have returned to an elder brother's house, although if it was to Ohrdruf that Bach did first return one could understand how his brother's keyboard MSS came to include certain music: eleven works by Georg Böhm, a few by Böhm's predecessor in Lüneburg, and a group of pieces by Lebègue, Dieupart, Lully, Marchand and Marais – the kind of French music, much of it up to date, known to Böhm and brought back by the young Bach. Extant manuscripts lead one to suppose that he also brought back chorale settings by the northerners, now lost, though contacts between organists and musicians were so many and so effective that rarely can one say how any of them got to know the music they copied.

The Sangerhausen job in 1702 fell through, for against the church authorities who favoured Bach, the reigning duke – perhaps the son of the same Duke of Weissenfels who had been impressed by the child Handel (see Mainwaring 1760, p. 9) – let it be known, with the force of a decree, that he preferred another, better-experienced candidate. Some thirty-five years later, history worked one of its ironies: in this fine church, Sebastian's third son, Johann Gottfried Bernhard Bach, not yet twenty-two, was recommended by his father and became organist, though alas not with long-lasting success (see below, p. 138).

Probably from Christmas 1702, and certainly for the first five months of 1703, Bach was serving at Weimar as 'court musician' (the genealogical table says 'Hofmusikant'). How or when he applied is not known for certain – presumably when the Sangerhausen appointment fell through in November 1702 – nor what instruments he played, nor whether he was able to use his knowledge of French styles: one can only guess that he played in both secular entertainments and chapel music, both violin and keyboard. His duties may have been such as to justify his next employers referring to him as 'Princely Saxon Court Organist' ('Fürstlich

Sächsischer HoffOrganiste': Dok II, p. 10), but in the accounts he is listed as 'Laquey', and perhaps had lowly servant duties in addition to playing violin and keyboards, copying music, substituting as organist and so forth. It is not unlikely that he applied for the Eisenach Georgen-kirche job when J. C. Bach died the following April, but the church was surely too important for an eighteen-year-old.

Although he soon left to take on a new organist's position in Arn-stadt, Bach had been part of an interesting musical establishment in Weimar, participating in the junior duke's private *cappella*, presumably with experienced musicians of the main ensemble. These included the violinist Johann Paul von Westhoff, who had published a set of solo violin suites in 1696: charming fiddle music of undoubted influence on Bach's later *Sei solo* for violin, lacking the heavy suavity of Bach's but with a sure sense of violin sound. Also in Weimar was the organist Johann Effler, to replace whom Bach returned as *Hoforganist* five years later. Though he may have substituted for Effler during this earlier period at the Weimar court, there is probably something *un peu arriviste* in Bach's calling himself 'princely court organist' when he next applied for a job, though presumably he did so for the sake of a church committee who would not be happy appointing a *Laquey*-fiddler as their new organist.

The following year [August 1703] he took on the duty of organist at the New Church in Arnstadt. Here indeed he showed the first fruits of his industry in the art of organ playing and in composition, the latter of which he had learnt chiefly through observing the works of the then most famous and thorough composers, and applying his own contemplation to them.

Presumably there was good reason to leave a court to become organist in a second-rank town church: for greater independence, double pay, likely additional fees, less demanding schedule, a preference for church music, more work with the organ, proximity to other family members, and potential students. Since Bach was already known in Arnstadt, perhaps the Weimar court job had been temporary? The Obituary's sentence implies that having been an orchestral player he was now for the first time able to develop as an organist, for which position he had qualified himself by careful study. But this suits its picture of an ideal church musician too well to be reliable, and a likely attraction in Arnstadt was its minor court and the chance of paid work there, in chamber music of various kinds.

As well as a new organ that drew him to the church, there were family connections: his grandfather had worked here, he was himself succeeded in 1708 by his cousin Johann Ernst, and the burgomaster in charge of the organ project was a brother-in-law of the Christoph Bach admired by Sebastian. This burgomaster had brought Bach in to test the new organ of the New Church (Bonifatiuskirche), perhaps on Christoph's recommendation as one more familiar than other local musicians with the great organs of Lüneburg and Hamburg – and as 'court organist to the princely court in Weimar', one able to judge the work of a builder thirty years his senior? Bach played J. F. Wender's new organ at its dedication, probably in early July 1703, with the usual hymns and perhaps some improvised solos. His agreed salary was fifty guilders for four services per week, against twenty for ten services paid to the interim organist Andreas Börner, whom he replaced and whose wife was one of his distant cousins. Fifty guilders was half the sum paid to the superintendent himself, who no doubt had access to other fees that were not available to his eighteen-year-old organist.

The instrument had twenty-three stops, pedal and two manuals, and was spread against the back wall of the church, high up in the third gallery, with a bigger bass sound than comparable instruments in north Germany, and tuned so as to allow most keys. Its builder was highly respected in the province. Such an organ, new and one hopes in faultless condition, was indeed such as would encourage a young composer. One can guess that here he wrote organ music of a kind familiar from the so-called Neumeister collection (shortish chorale settings harmonising the melodies in a variety of textures), some longer chorale fantasias with more distinct sections, variations on chorales (music also suiting the harpsichord), and preludes or toccatas in various sections. Such secular works as the Capriccio in B flat major BWV 992, picturing in six movements the events around someone departing on a journey, show him to have assimilated the style of programmatic or story-telling sonatas recently published in Leipzig by Johann Kuhnau.

Other works suggest an intimate grasp of other idioms, such as Georg Böhm's toccata-like preludes and Pachelbel's fluent counterpoint, each of which informed many a Bach work of the same kind.

By 'the then most famous and thorough [gründlichen] composers' the Obituary was probably implying those mentioned in the next section, below: worthy composers the opposite of frivolous, trained to handle harmony expertly. But a prime influence was also the more local Thuringian composers, including his father-in-law-to-be Johann Michael Bach, whose chorale settings, though almost totally free of harmonic tension or inspired melody, are literate and at times hard to distinguish from the young Sebastian's. There are signs throughout his life that Bach was responding to – striving to do better than – local composers, minor talents who could have been seen throughout his life as in some sense competitors. Examples are Buttstedt or C. F. Hurlebusch for fugues, Daniel Vetter for chorales, J. P. von Westhoff and J. G. Graun for violin music, G. F. Kauffmann and Walther for chorale collections. Similarly, it seems unlikely that cantatas of Telemann or J. C. Graupner would not be standing behind his later Weimar work, influencing them if only negatively. Later still, there are clear responses to the more galant music of his elder sons and their contemporaries.

Whatever gifts Bach developed at Arnstadt, he did so beyond the requirements of his position in the second church of the town, where he had to play only chorales (with their preludes?) at four services per week. When on several counts he was interrogated formally in 1705 and 1706, he was asked why he performed no ensemble music with the student singers and players (Dok II, pp. 20–1), and his answer, in stating a desire for a competent director, implied that he would not play with an incompetent. He added that he would also answer this particular question in writing but how truculent these replies actually were is impossible to say, since the clerk was reporting only the gist.

Perhaps Bach was being discreet and would not criticise a colleague to a committee. Since ensemble music was not in his contract he was certainly within his rights not to play, and in this respect was setting a pattern for protecting those rights throughout his career. A director, not an organist, would be responsible for ensemble music, and no doubt appropriately paid – perhaps Bach was looking for promotion now he was nearly twenty-one? That from the beginning he must have bargained for a good salary (as an erstwhile 'organist to the princely court', poached by Arnstadt?) is suggested by the pay of his eventual successor being only 80 per cent of his.

The consistory court, including superintendent J. G. Olearius (one of a family of distinguished clergy), had other problems with their organist, as courts often do with young people. Here, they centred on the way he fulfilled his duties and on his relations with the student players serving Arnstadt's musical needs, with whom Bach, younger than many of them, apparently did not get on well. In 1705 there was a brawl in the marketplace, in the course of which he behaved 'like a dog's etc.', drew a rapier and called one J. H. Geyersbach a 'Zippel Fagottist' (*Dok* II, p. 16). Quite what was reprehensible about this is unclear. 'Zippel' could be a dialect version of 'discipulus', so Geyersbach, who was three years older, was being called a 'learner bassoonist' by a junior. But 'Zippel' also meant the male member (Marshall 2000, p. 501); and 'Fagott' might have circulated *sub rosa* to mean homosexual, as it seems to have done from the days when Bosch painted a woodwind instrument protruding *ex ano* (*Garden of Delights*, *c*1500) through to modern American slang. So was it an offensive pun? The incident came to court because Bach asked for protection, thus going on the offensive to accuse Geyersbach, despite admitting that he was wearing a rapier – which, by the way, suggests that he may have come in uniform from some Arnstadt court music that evening (Wolff 2000, p. 87).

There was also the impropriety of allowing a girl into the choir gallery and letting her take part in the music: 'die frembde Jungfer', usually translated as 'the strange' or 'unfamiliar maiden'. 'Jungfer' means she was unmarried, though it is unknown if this was Maria

Barbara, whom Bach married a year later, or her sister or someone else. But 'fremd' means 'unauthorised' not 'strange': she had not been authorised to enter the gallery or join the choir. Like other organists, Bach had signed a contract to keep the organ in good order and to admit no one to it, or presumably its gallery, without the knowledge of the superintendent (Dok II, p. 11). At Erfurt in 1678, Pachelbel had similarly signed a contract stipulating that 'no unauthorised person' was to touch the organ ('kein Frembder': DTÖ 17, p. viii). So there is less of a frisson about this famous incident than is often now assumed.

The Obituary did not mention such incidents, either not knowing them or, just as likely, doing as Emanuel later asked his biographer Forkel to do: pass over stories of 'his youthful pranks' (Dok III, p. 286). Quite why anecdotes were neglected is a question worth asking, however. Read properly, much can be learnt from them, incidents conveying better than anything else the impression of a lively young man, and giving a glimpse of what today's biographies look for. But anecdotes would have worked against the image Emanuel Bach was presenting.

In the arts of the organ he took for himself works of Bruhns,
Reinken, Buxtehude and some good French organists as models.

As is clear from his brother's albums (see above, p. 17), these names are likely to have featured in Sebastian's studies, from MSS he brought back to Thuringia or regularly circulating amongst musicians. But by the time the Obituary authors heard him speak of composers he admired, these names had a higher reputation than such local composers as Kuhnau, whom he had also certainly once imitated. Even Bruhns, whose music was the least well known, had become familiar after the stories told about him by Mattheson in his book of 1740. In addition, Emanuel notes that his father's favourites, appropriately for a hero-composer, were all strong fugue composers (Dok III, p. 288). A question still not fully answered is how much more relevant great composers such as Buxtehude were to Bach's earliest works – such as Cantatas 150, 71 and 106, which tunefully adopt traditional genres – than local composers. The layout of Cantata 71, for example, with its choruses of woodwind, brass, strings and choir, could have been prompted by the polychoral performances of Buxtehude (whose Marienkirche still has its separate minstrel galleries such as encouraged stereophony) but also by more local traditions going back a century or more.

From various sources, it seems that French organists with whose works J. S. Bach became familiar (in part) before his later twenties include Raison, d'Anglebert, Boyvin, Dieupart, Du Mage, de Grigny and Marchand, but exactly when in each case is less certain. Did he know Raison's *Premier livre* of 1688 while still at Arnstadt, a book which surely gave him the fugue subject and possibly the whole ostinato theme of the organ passacaglia? In the case of non-keyboard music, an intimate understanding of French *manière* can be traced later: music such as the Ouverture of Cantata 61 (1714) probably had little to do with organ music, French or Thuringian, though both of its movements paraphrase the chorale melody. Rather, a cantata would gather together all and any kinds of musical idiom, for the greater glory but also for the musical challenge of it: applying modern French rhythms in the accompaniment to an old German chorale melody is exactly the mixing of styles to which Bach was attracted from first to last.

In a letter of 1775 Emanuel names none of the French composers 'loved and studied' by his father, despite citing no fewer than nine Germans in one sentence: Froberger, Kerll, Pachelbel, J. K. F. Fischer, N. A. Strunck, Buxtehude, Reinken, Bruhns and Böhm (*Dok* III, p. 288). This again is rather of a piece with the Obituary's disdain for the Parisian virtuoso Louis Marchand (see below, p. 73). Furthermore, true though it could well be that Emanuel's father and uncle admired those particular German composers, it is also the case that in 1752 Emanuel's Berlin colleague Joachim Quantz had published a similar list of the 'famous men' who had benefited from assimilating Italian and French tastes. They had developed the art of organ playing beyond the Netherlanders, and this was an art that culminated in J. S. Bach. The last point is one reconveyed by both the Obituary and Emanuel's own treatise the *Versuch*, which was either prompted by Quantz's book or reaffirming it.

Emanuel does mention one non-German organist by name, Frescobaldi, some of whose music probably penetrated to Thuringia before
Bach acquired a copy of Fiori musicali (dated by him 1714 and known to
Emanuel?), and who had long been a big influence on German composers. Perhaps Legrenzi, Corelli and Albinoni are not mentioned by
the Obituary because they were forgotten in Germany by c1750, or, just
as likely, because Emanuel knew few early works of his father which
used their themes and structures. Perhaps there were also nationalistic
reasons: Emanuel does not mention Vivaldi either, although sudden
acquaintance with various Vivaldi concertos had changed his father's
ideas for ever. Or, finally, perhaps working on themes by other composers was something Emanuel's generation no longer admired, although it had long been rather a central German habit, one in the light
of which Handel's lifelong habit of purloining can be viewed.

At a certain moment here in Arnstadt he had so strong an urge
to hear as many good organists as he could that he set out for
Lübeck, actually on foot, in order to hear the famous organist
of St Mary's, Dietrich Buxtehude, and stayed there not without
benefit for almost a quarter of a year. Then he returned
to Arnstadt.

Here, in further testimony to Bach the self-taught master, one senses
in the words 'so strong an urge' the composer's own sentiments, even
perhaps his words. 'At a certain moment' also raises the vision of a
young man of initiative who found his first appointment a little too
constricting. Curiously, although it says 'many good organists', only
Buxtehude is mentioned by name, and the reader has to infer that there
were possibly others. Even though Emanuel is unlikely to have known
that Bach was criticised on his return by his employers, there is still a
sense here of the artist disregarding whatever stood in the way of his
art. Setting out on foot to increase one's learning was not something
despised in the period of the German Enlightenment. Was the phrase
'on foot' meant to contrast with the picture recently given of Handel's

apparently warmer reception at Lübeck in 1703 (Mattheson 1740, p. 94)? Either way, in c1705 both Hamburg and Lübeck were known to other musicians from the Bach–Handel region: J. C. Schieferdecker (from Weissenfels), C. Graupner (a Leipziger) and the J. C. Bach described in the genealogical table as fond of travelling (Dok I, p. 200).

A careful reader, however, might have wondered why Bach did not go straight from Lüneburg to study with Buxtehude, or – once again – to Nuremberg to study with his brother's teacher and sister's godfather, Pachelbel. But Pachelbel himself, in the preface to his *Hexachordum Apollinis* (1699), had mentioned Buxtehude as one of two possible teachers for his son Wilhelm, aged thirteen, and such publications were still known half a century later. Either way, the reverence attaching to Buxtehude seems proverbial. As for Bach, though it was not unknown for the young organist of a modest town to go far to experience the best in his profession, nor was it quite ordinary either, and his prolonged absence from Arnstadt raises the question whether he went to Lübeck at least in part to look for a job.

In February 1706 the Arnstadt consistory court summoned Bach to explain why he had been absent for four times as long as the month he had been allowed by the superintendent for a study trip 'to understand one thing or another in his art' (Dok II, p. 19). But if, on 18 October, he really had set out on foot, he could not possibly have journeyed to Lübeck, undertaken studies, and then journeyed back all within a month; nor would he have been able to hear Buxtehude's mixed sacred concerts over the Advent period, which were surely part of the point. So had he intended to deceive? Not the least interesting word in Bach's explanation was 'art' ('Kunst'), the new shibboleth excusing all. But the court must have wished that his *Kunst* had indeed been improved, for it reprimanded him further, complaining that

> until now [about 2 February 1706] he had been making many odd
> *variationes* in the hymns, mixing up in it many strange keys [*Thone*], so
> that the congregation became confused by it. In future, if he wants to

bring in a wandering key [tonum peregrinum], he has to stay with it and not turn conspicuously to something else too quickly or, as he has so far been used to doing, even playing in some contrary key [Tonum contrarium]. (Dok II, p. 20)

Obviously the clerk and/or the non-musicians present were using technical terms loosely. 'Tonus peregrinus', for example, does not mean the particular modal melody with this name to which the Magnificat was often sung. But the main lines of the complaint are clear enough: a young organist was wilfully or otherwise annoying the clergy and people with over-adventurous harmonies of a kind unsuitable for a modest parish church, and they knew enough to be able to specify what they did not like.

The adverbs 'until now' or 'so far' ('bißher') suggest that Bach had been offending in this way before he ever went to Lübeck. It is quite possible that some extant chorale settings, even if too confidently called 'Arnstadt Chorales' by later scholars, do represent the kind of gratuitous chromaticism liked by some organists in Thuringia in the period around 1700. The hymns were after all very familiar, frequently sung and memorised, and often with many more verses than is acceptable today, so some variety introduced by the organist was not unreasonable. (Even now, many organists find interfering with a hymn's basic harmonies, epecially in a final verse, irresistible.) And as well as giving variety, wandering keys and/or unexpected harmonies were a standard means of responding to the text. Words of penitence, for example, would draw from the organist a descending chromatic line (this is something always easy to introduce), words of hope an ascending chromatic line, and so on. Many of Bach's later Orgelbüchlein settings, written while he was court organist at Weimar and containing some of the most beautiful music in the organist's repertory, still explore such 'affective' devices. And although no doubt they do this subtly, some of the Orgelbüchlein settings would also have startled and upset an ordinary parish-church congregation.

And there was a further complaint:

> so far Bach had played somewhat too long, but after an indication of this was given him by the superintendent, he had immediately fallen into the other extreme and had made it too short.

Since the original complaint was made by his choir prefect, a student of comparable age, it seems that there were bad relations between them. Was the prefect in league with the superintendent? Had he politely remonstrated and met with aggression from the organist? 'Too long' and 'too short' must apply to organ preludes, but preludes to what exactly is unknown: to the service as a whole (the opening voluntary), to the congregation's hymns, or (as likely) to ensemble music for which the performers needed time to group, tune, etc.? A long-lasting quarrel thirty years later in Leipzig also concerned Bach's bad relations with a choir prefect, though in neither case is it clear whether the reason was personal (some incompatability), professional (the prefects were not good enough), or formal (they were not of his choosing but of the clergy's). Whichever it was, it would have been exacerbated by any natural contrariness in Bach's nature, such as is all too evident in the present incident: first he played too long, then too short.

What part exactly the Lübeck visit of 1705–6 contributed to the composer's maturing grasp of musical language and form can only be guessed. Buxtehude's pleasing harmony, charming melody and clever counterpoint must have been in particular evidence in his church concerts, whose scope, planning and standards of performance were famous. Of the two pieces known to have been performed in December 1705 (BuxWV 134 and 135), the latter had a violin or string ensemble of twenty-five, probably the biggest that Bach had ever heard. He seems to have responded to Buxtehude's multi-section praeludia for organ much as the younger Italian violin composers responded to the works of their predecessors: by developing the many short sections towards separate longer movements. In Bach's case, this meant making from the various short sections of the old toccatas and sonatas fewer movements but each of a more rounded, sustained, free-standing shape. Buxtehude's melodic gifts were inspiring, in both short chorales and longer fantasias whose sections are much like those of string sonatas. No home-grown Thuringian composer often went beyond conventional formulas to create new, winsome melodies from old hymn tunes, as Buxtehude did.

Perhaps Bach was particularly taken with Buxtehude's passacaglias (including those in lost choral works?), bringing three of them back for his brother to copy into the ongoing Andreas Bach Book and at some point responding to them by creating his own Passacaglia in C minor for organ, drawing on two themes of André Raison. But this Passacaglia turns out to be more sustained, organised and thorough than any possible models, German, French or Italian, almost as if Bach were consciously running through the many keyboard patterns familiar to organists. Perhaps he was, just as in the Passacaglia's fugue he explores, at unheard-of length, traditional permutation techniques (using three themes in various vertical combinations). Length itself seems to have interested both the young Bach and Handel, even in genres such as suite dances that had usually been cast as modest binary movements. The thoroughness with which Bach handles so many compositional problems is already shown, at a naive level, in some early works – by the way he runs through changing time signatures in the little prelude BWV 921, for example, or through changing textures in the organ chorale BWV 739. The approach is fertile, imaginative, even alarmingly obsessive: a combination that can be glimpsed throughout his life.

The complaints about Bach at Arnstadt ring true for a young composer of wide horizons and promising talent. While a young man, his study of music from distant cultures – Corelli, Antonio Biffi, Reinken – suggests a deeply creative interest in counterpoint beyond the requirements of a Thuringian parish church's music, and one would like to know how much of it he came across by chance and by design. Various contrapuntal devices were explored by Albinoni, Corelli and Legrenzi (combination of different themes), as by Biffi (a theme overlapping itself), suggesting that this was the attraction for the young Bach. It was 'interesting music' worth studying and imitating.[1] But what the good people of Arnstadt New Church wanted was for their organist to play over the hymn tune straightforwardly – 'thematicè', as Pachelbel's contract in Erfurt had it – so that they knew what and when to sing.

In 1707 he was called as organist to St Blasius, Mühlhausen.

Since Buxtehude was not far from seventy years old in 1705, Bach may well have gone to Lübeck to solicit his job in the huge, majestic Marienkirche, with its outstanding organs (one of them with over fifty stops) and its famously active musical life. One is bound to wonder whether any such idea came to nothing for the same scurrilous reason Mattheson gave as to why neither he nor Handel wished to succeed Buxtehude: they could not accept the 'marriage condition' (1740, p. 94), which was to marry Buxtehude's eldest daughter, ten years older than either Handel or Bach. Buxtehude's eventual successor did marry her, as her father had married his predecessor Tunder's daughter. Apprentices or successors often married the master's daughter or widow, as if they were becoming a 'partner' to 'take over the family business', one with assured income and legally entitled fees. Why Mattheson, Handel and Bach all declined, if they did, one can only guess.

A month after the Arnstadt court's complaint of November 1706 about the 'unauthorised maiden', the organist of St Blasius ('Divi Blasii') in Mühlhausen died, and by the following April Bach was auditioning for the position, having been informed or encouraged again by local contacts. Mühlhausen had many connections with Hamburg, personal, commercial and presumably musical, and its potential must have seemed superior to Arnstadt's. A major city, it had a proud position in Reformation history and boasted over a dozen churches, including the two big Gothic structures of St Mary and St Blasius. But by Bach's time it was marked by a High/Low Church factiousness, orthodox versus Pietist, the latter of which was likely to prefer simpler music. Although

---

[1] So too the quadruple invertible counterpoint in Vivaldi's D minor concerto was doubtless an attraction for Bach when he later transcribed it for organ (BWV 596).

Forkel, guessing or passing on something Emanuel had told him, said that Bach received several offers about this time (1802, p. 6), the only certainty is the invitation of Advent 1706 to test a new village organ near Gehren, where there were more Bachs. Perhaps for some time he had been searching for wider horizons than Arnstadt gave him – either this or Forkel had some inkling of The Problem of Buxtehude's Daughter.

'To be called as organist' is the usual formula, less pretentious than the modern professional's claim to being 'head-hunted'. In some sense not now clear, Bach competed with others for the post in Mühlhausen, a more important church than St Boniface, Arnstadt, where his position had been a new one. J. G. Walther also applied at Mühlhausen but (on Bach's urging?) withdrew, being appointed to the town church of Weimar by the end of July that year, soon after that to be a colleague of Bach's there. At Mühlhausen, it seems certain that music for the audition included one or two cantatas. Bach's, sung on Easter Sunday 1707, was therefore quite possibly Cantata 4, an early work both appropriate to the day and, as a set of variations on the hymn, particularly intelligible to a committee. Bach shook hands on 15 June, obtained dismissal from Arnstadt on 29 June, returned the organ keys there, and apparently began at Mühlhausen on 1 July.

The previous organists, J. G. Ahle and his father, were distinguished citizens of Mühlhausen, and since Bach's salary was higher by more than 30 per cent – his predecessors had probably had other forms of employment too – what he could offer the church and town must have been recognised. Although his contract did not specify the production of cantatas, only to perform his duties 'willingly' and be available at all times (Dok II, p. 24), the organist of St Blasius supplied at least one great celebratory piece each year: a cantata for St Mary's on the election of the town council. In February 1708 Cantata 71 was performed and actually printed in movable type – not only the text but (on Bach's urging?) the work's nineteen vocal and instrumental parts – a cantata at times much like Buxtehude's though not quite as light of touch. In addition, he was to have duties at several other churches in the city, all together amounting to some six regular weekly services, plus weddings and funerals, at which he mostly played hymns and organ music based on them. The autograph score of Cantata 131 carries a note that it was composed 'at the desire of G. C. Eilmar', archdeacon at St Mary's and a known antagonist of the superintendent of Bach's church. Both it and Cantata 71 show an increasing grasp of how cantatas of several movements can be built, with a virtually *ad hoc* sequence of introductions, choral songs, arias, chorales, interludes and so on, now contrapuntal, now homophonic, the whole informed by particular images in the words. Neither No. 131 nor No. 71 yet contains Italian recitative, but there are antiphonal choruses, constantly changing textures, brief instrumental solos, polychoral instrumentation (brass+drums, strings, reeds, recorders), SATB solos, fugue, permutation fugue, aria and duet aria. The whole is often short-phrased or even short-breathed, recalling (especially in No. 131) earlier German music such as Schütz's but lacking the dazzling expanse of form and melody achieved by Handel in Italy at about the same period ('Dixit Dominus', 'Laudate, pueri'). Yet there is in Cantata 71 a freshness missing from the more run-of-the-mill Italian imitations of the day. The very range of Italian tempo words in the score shows Bach wishing to air his increasing but still youthful knowledge.

Two other aspects of Bach's musical life in Mühlhausen throw some light on his activities. The first is his taking on pupils: various reports speak of J. M. Schubart studying with him from 1707 to 1717 (Walther 1732, p. 557), and of J. C. Vogler from the Arnstadt period onwards – significant, since they were Bach's first and second successor at Weimar respectively. Doubtless there were other pupils, and we know of these two only because they seem to have served as apprentice-like assistants.

The second activity is organ advising. In February 1708, his plans for a newly rebuilt organ in 'Divi Blasii' were presented, and the builder J. F. Wender undertook the work, as one of several organs he built in the neighbourhood. Perhaps Wender had been active in getting Bach the Mühlhausen job, knowing him from Arnstadt and collaborating with him on some other organ examinations not now documented.

Instigating a significant organ project only half a year after taking up his position suggests no ordinary, twenty-two-year-old musician.

Like Kuhnau and others drawing up organ schemes, Bach seems to have described the Mühlhausen organ's faults and remedies, when he came to put pen to paper, mainly on the basis of what he read in Andreas Werckmeister's *Orgelprobe* (enlarged edition, 1698), and a big question remains as to how expert in organ building he actually was, whatever his later admirers said. A university-educated musician such as Kuhnau would hardly have considered a craftsman's technicalities to be in his purview, and would automatically have consulted a book, especially one as recent, 'local' and full of good sense as Werckmeister's. So might Bach have done.

One scrutinises Bach's reports for signs of intimate technical knowledge without very much success. Thus although at Mühlhausen he is now said to have 'missed hardly any minutiae' and even mentioned pipe materials (Wolff 2000, pp. 143–4), in fact the details he stipulated – 'fourteen-ounce tin' for the case pipes, some 'good wood' for an accompanying stop, presumably meaning oak – needed no more than elementary knowledge. Nor, ten years later, did specifying a lighter touch and shallower keyfall in the Leipzig Paulinerkirche report (Dok I, p. 164) need much more: these wished-for improvements may not even have been practical at that stage. It also seems to be the case that when in 1746 the organist at the Wenzelskirche, Naumburg, reported on all the faults in the new organ recently approved by Bach and the privileged organ builder of Saxony, Gottfried Silbermann, he was implying – for whatever reason – that the two examiners had done their job only superficially (Dok II, pp. 429–31).

Nevertheless, in conforming with Werckmeister's model stoplist and following much of his advice, Bach's scheme at Mühlhausen is well conceived and succinctly presented, with the salient points grasped and made clear. The musical potential of what he was recommending was very promising, thanks probably to good use being made of Werckmeister's various recommendations: bellows and chests must be remade for both bigger capacity and evenness of wind; a good sub-suboctave bass must be introduced in the pedal, to give a good founda-tion; the reed stops need to be improved (their timbre modernised?), as does the Tremulant; a twenty-six-bell Glockenspiel is desired (for the upper half of the keyboard?) plus some new colour stops (Viola 8′, Nassat 3′, a Fagott 16′ for ensemble music); there needs to be a thorough tuning (temperament not specified); and finally, the organ needs a complete new third manual or *Brustwerk*.

This last would have been largely for accompaniment of the con-tinuo kind and playing occasional solos in ensemble music. It would be located just above the heads of the players in the spacious west-end gallery. Between c1690, when the organ had last been radically worked on, and 1707, therefore, either the rôle of the organ in such a church had broadened or its new organist had new ambitions. Curiously, Bach says nothing about the action, though a new chest – a *Brustwerk*, placed above the other two – ideally meant remade keyboards and playing mechanism. Can he really have taken it for granted that the keyboard touch and action would be good, or was he not particularly fastidious about such things?

There is a possibility that the chorale 'Ein feste Burg' BWV 720 was written for this organ. But the extant copy's details are typical of its writer (J. G. Walther) and have no certain authority. Nor are its registrations more specific to this organ than to so many others of that time and place, including Walther's own.

> Twice our Bach was married. The first time [on Monday 17 October 1707] was with Miss Maria Barbara Bach, the youngest daughter of Johann Michael Bach, a good composer. By her he had seven children, namely five sons and two daughters, amongst whom was a pair of twins.

With her sisters, Maria Barbara Bach had been living in Arnstadt since the death of their mother in 1704, probably with the family of the burgomaster, a relation. She and Sebastian were related, sharing a great-grandfather, Johannes (†1626). Her father is represented by some chorales in the Neumeister collection, and it is possible he had some influence on Sebastian's development, or at least on his early work in local kinds of chorale setting. No doubt, too, Emanuel liked to have it on record that his own maternal grandfather was a good musician, as his mother is also likely to have been.

The marriage took place in Dornheim, a village church near Arnstadt, where the pastor was a family friend. This was two months after Bach received a bequest of fifty guilders from his Erfurt uncle Tobias Lämmerhirt, in memory of whom perhaps the exquisite Cantata 106 was composed. (This is another sectional work sustained by a sure sense of melody, not least when a typical scoring of the day, such as the opening recorders and gambas, is rethought in the composer's increasingly distinctive style.) Nothing is known of the wedding itself, although many members of the greater Bach family lived within convenient distance. Both the Wedding Cantata 196 and the suggestive Quodlibet BWV 524 may have been involved in the wedding, the first in the service (and/or at the pastor's own marriage service some months later?), the second in the kind of rowdy family gathering glimpsed in some later reports, when they wished to draw a picture of a 'human Bach'.

The children of Sebastian and Maria Barbara Bach were as follows:

* Catharina Dorothea, Weimar, 29 December 1708
* Wilhelm Friedemann, Weimar, 22 November (St Cecilia's Day) 1710
Maria Sophia and Johann Christoph, twins, 23 February 1713, did not survive
* Carl Philipp Emanuel, Weimar, 8 March 1714
Johann Gottfried Bernhard, Weimar, 11 May 1715
Leopold Augustus, Cöthen, 15 November 1718, died within a year

The Obituary listed the children still living (*) and gave the two sons' current positions, but no further details. Only a formal document or two cast any light at all on personal matters. Thus a census reveals that Maria Barbara's elder stepsister Friedelena Margaretha Bach lived with them, from about the time the first child was born, it is thought (Dok II, p. 39). Like many an unmarried sister, she was probably the housekeeper, remaining so until she died in 1729, well after Bach's marriage to Anna Magdalena, to be replaced as housekeeper by Maria Barbara's daughter Catharina Dorothea. The baptism register in Cöthen, where Leopold Augustus was born, suggests that his death at ten months was not foreseen, as must often have been the case: the five godparents were the prince, his sister, his brother and two high-ranking courtiers (Dok II, p. 73). How distressing Leopold's and the twins' deaths were, or how comforting Friedelena's presence was, no one now knows, but Emanuel's reference to the twins suggests an abiding family sadness.

3 Weimar, 1708–1717

In the following year [1708], a visit he made to Weimar, and the
opportunity he had to be heard there by the then duke, led to a
post being offered him as the chamber and court organist.

Twelve months after he was appointed at Mühlhausen and without
waiting for the rebuilt organ to be finished, Bach moved to Weimar,
where Maria Barbara gave birth to their first child. He had visited
Weimar in June 1708, when the organ was being worked on, and on
25 June wrote a formal request for release from Mühlhausen (Dok I,
pp. 19–20). Was it family lore that Bach was heard by chance in Weimar
by the duke? – it would explain why he took another job so soon. While
a duke would appoint without the need to invite applications, hold auditions or have candidates vetted by committees, a post could not have
been offered unless it was vacant or about to become so. This suggests
one of two things: either that the 'visit he made to Weimar' was undertaken by Bach in the knowledge that Johann Effler was retiring from
the position; or that in visiting Weimar (in a capacity now unknown) to
review work on the organ, he learnt of Effler's intentions, put himself
forward as successor and was auditioned by the duke. The Obituary
seems to want to imply the latter, but would not know the full story.

Bach's request for release from Mühlhausen is the document of an
astute man, one keen to score more points than was necessary, perhaps

aware that his departure was earlier than decorum required. It speaks first of his gratitude for the Mühlhausen appointment, then of his wish to have created a well-regulated church music ('wohlzufassenden kirchenmusic') such as, he says, was then becoming known in every town. This must refer to cantatas, for which he needed the larger organ described in the last chapter, and was a concept ('well-regulated church music') he returned to many years later in Leipzig. The document then goes on to relate ways in which he had performed beyond the obligations of duty, namely by building a library of the 'choicest cantatas' ('auserlessensten kirchen Stücken') and by drawing up the organ project. He twice speaks of experiencing 'hindrance' and 'vexation' ('wiedrigkeit', 'verdriessligkeit') in his job, despite support from many people in his church, and adds that in any case he needs a position with better pay. Finally, God brought it about that he has had an offer at Weimar as court and chamber musician (he does not say organist), where he has hopes for a church music of the kind he described. This sounds as if he was expecting to have the opportunity at Weimar to compose cantatas and other ensemble music, though he had to wait another eight years for this. 'Chamber musician' would be a grander appointment than 'court musician', indicating membership of the more select group providing regular and private music for the duke, rather than the merely ceremonial and public music. Was he exaggerating the importance of the position he was going to, as at Arnstadt the importance of the one he was coming from?

Marriage and impending fatherhood must have made better pay desirable, and it is possible that Maria Barbara's condition had prompted him to visit Weimar. Or there were problems with the Mühlhausen clergy, for the Low Church pastor of his church, J. A. Frohne, is likely to have been against the very kind of 'well-regulated' ensemble music his organist wanted. Or there were tensions between the two main churches' clergy themselves, perhaps a particular falling out that year over a cantata for 24 June, St John's day (Petzoldt 2000, p. 187). Or Bach did not get on well with the instrumentalists in Mühlhausen and/or preferred the potential of a court's music making to that of a parish church. Certainly the musical possibilities in Weimar were greater, and it is the case that Bach, like clergymen, was called by God only to a higher position. The request for dismissal can certainly be read as having touches of self-excuse and disingenuousness, or at least a barb or two thrown by the departing.

Weimar, though much smaller than Mühlhausen, was a German 'residence city', or seat of an absolute ruler, in whose cultural life music featured high, judging by a succession of well-known musicians who had worked there: M. Vulpius, J. H. Schein, Schütz (for a short time), J. G. Walther, and Bach himself some years previously. (Much later in Weimar, Bach seems to have been largely forgotten. George Eliot, who stayed there in the 1850s, does not mention him.) But whatever the reasons for leaving Mühlhausen, personal and professional contacts there did not cease: the Marienkirche's archdeacon and his daughter were each a godparent to Bach's first two children, and he was asked to return to the city both to check on the organ project in the other church and to supply election cantatas in 1709 and 1710. Also, years later he was evidently welcomed when accompanying his son Johann Gottfried Bernhard on the boy's successful application at the Marienkirche in 1735.

Letting himself be heard playing in Weimar, presumably in the court chapel rather than the town church, sounds like suing for patronage, and he must have made a good impression. As reported above, young Handel was also heard by a duke as he played the organ in his chapel (Mainwaring 1760, p. 9), in this case the Duke of Weissenfels: was it a standard way of obtaining a ruler's attention, in Handel's case not for a job but some other kind of patronage? At Weimar, by 20 June Bach's salary was approved and he was paid in part for the second quarter of 1708, at a rate nearly double that of Mühlhausen, and received an *ex gratia* payment for removal expenses. As at any court, the hiring and firing of employees was not an open process, and the duke's appointment specifies little more than terms of payment, including corn, barley and beer allowances (Küster 1996, pp. 186–7).

By 14 July 1708, the Bachs were resident in Weimar and the Mühlhausen church had a successor in place. Listed as 'court organist', Bach was much better paid than most parish church organists, with a rise in salary in 1711, and again on promotion in March 1714, and lived in a fellow court musician's house. One particularly kindred spirit at court, so one can guess, was the volinist J. G. Pisendel, and there may have been good contact with Telemann, then in Eisenach and already a man of wide experience, not least in Leipzig where he had been a student. Bach's relative J. G. Walther (teacher of one of the scions of the ducal house, Prince Johann Ernst) was organist of the church to whose parish the young Bach family probably belonged. Doubtless less self-reliant than Bach, Walther seems to have been a much more prolific copyist of other people's organ music than was the new court organist, and owned a great deal of organ music in manuscript. To judge by French, Italian and German works which each of them owned or copied in Weimar, there was a lively exchange of musical ideas between the two organists. (How unusual this was is difficult to know, since it was the Bach name that led to so many musical sources surviving into the age of antiquarian collectors.) Other acquaintances of theirs in Weimar, such as J. C. Vogler, also copied French music, and the young prince himself composed concertos imitating Vivaldi with a competence that was rare for noblemen, if not unique.

'Chamber musician' indicated duties in the general music making at court. Whether they included solo harpsichord playing cannot now be known, and only guesses can be made about the genres of chamber music then fashionable and in which Bach presumably participated: solo sonatas (violin, gamba, recorder), string and mixed trios, broken consort music for wind, strings and keyboard – works Italians called concertos. Various such groups are glimpsed in several Weimar cantatas, springs from which the mighty stream of instrumental groupings for the Brandenburg Concertos issued later (see below). Cantata 18, which also includes the new recitative, uses four solo violas for a sound and texture all its own, and one cannot be sure that such cantatas were performed only in chapel. There seems every reason to suppose that the

Weimar musicians built on the tradition for mixed consorts to create newer works in a wide variety of instrumental combinations.

Although the sources do not show it, some instrumental works known in arrangements for Leipzig church cantatas (Nos. 146, 156, 188, 35) or as Leipzig harpsichord concertos (the D minor solo, the C major triple) may have originated for other forces in Weimar concerts during Bach's later years there.

No sources or surviving versions exist to clarify this picture, which is a great pity since it would illustrate a phase in the composer's changing approach to his own music over his lifetime. For instance, the likelier that the bewitching Largo of the F minor harpsichord concerto goes back to a solo work of the Weimar period for oboe or recorder or violin, the likelier that its lovely, later scoring – pizzicato strings in A flat major, with a cantabile harpsichord solo – was aiming at a new and more striking *Affekt* than the original, and was doing so to touch the hearts of a larger concert public in Leipzig. Vivaldi's influence is to be heard in such pieces, and yet the result is distinct, with a spirit behind it that comes closer to a Weimar organ chorale such as 'Nun komm der Heiden Heiland' BWV 659a than it does to any Venetian concerto.

That in his life as a composer at the ducal court Bach was systematically studying the difference between Italian and French idioms is clear not only from his cantatas but also in the *Sei solo* for violin, discussed briefly below (p. 87). Whether or how well Bach played such solos himself is not known, though his violin playing is unlikely to have been neglected at Weimar. In 1713, a pupil, P. D. Kräuter, wrote about the French and Italian music that was being performed at court, following the young prince's recent return from Holland, and referred to being taught these styles by J. S. Bach (*Dok* III, p. 650). So the Obituary was not alone in wanting to establish its subject's credentials with respect to the French courtly styles of music. Especially in Weimar by c1715 there was ample opportunity for a wide repertory, and it could well be that the reason we know so little about this repertory is that the scores, both for the chamber and for the chapel music, were the duke's property, kept in his library, not allowed to be copied, and were unfortunately discarded or burnt in the fire of 1774 that destroyed the castle. The paper itself on which the music was written certainly belonged to the duke (see Dok II, p. 56).

His Grace's pleasure in his [Bach's] playing fired him up to attempt everything possible in the art of how to treat the organ. Here too he wrote the majority of his organ works [*Orgelstücke*].

Which of the two Weimar dukes this refers to, Wilhelm Ernst, the senior, or Ernst August, the junior, is not clear, and perhaps Emanuel did not know, though in 1775 it was the latter he cited as having particularly supported his father (Dok III, p. 289). Also, it was Ernst August's younger half-brother Johann Ernst whose string works are found amongst Bach's transcriptions. Either way, the Obituary is silent on one intractable problem of life in Weimar: the two dukes lived in such mutual enmity as would inevitably involve the chapel musicians in one way or another.

The chapel organ was in and out of commission from June 1712 to May 1714 and never became very grand. It and the musicians were located high in a sort of attic chamber 20 m above the chapel floor, occupying the space around a small balustraded opening in the ceiling, 4 m × 3 m, through which they looked and sounded down into the rectangular chapel, 30 m long and 12 m wide. This was occupied at various levels, ground floor and two running galleries, not by a parish congregation but by court personnel, who looked towards a liturgical east-end structure that was not unlike a stage set. This consisted of (in a vertical line from bottom to top) step, altar rail, altar table, baldacchino, pulpit, an obelisk pointing up to 'heaven's opening', then the attic gallery balustrade, some way behind it the organ, and then finally a fresco in the domed ceiling above. The organ, virtally at the peak of this 'path to heaven', was against the wall, with bass pipes and bellows chamber at the back. Originally it had one manual only (1658), which was probably all that could be accommodated comfortably in the space; but then a second was added, its chest of pipes placed to the side (a *Seitenwerk*) and played presumably by a complicated action that might well not have worked quite perfectly. Improvement was made in 1707–8 by relocating its chest under the main chest beyond or above its keyboard, and so turning it into an *Unterwerk*. Further work on the organ during Bach's term of office resulted in an enlarged chamber, bigger bass pipes and a row of tuned bells (probably for the manual's upper half, positioned just behind the music desk), the whole now comprising about two dozen stops. Quite why the Mühlhausen and Weimar organs needed a row of bells is never explained, and one can only conjecture that they sounded at certain jolly moments, during the organ's or the congregation's chorales at Christmas, perhaps. But the expense of brass (?) bells and faultless striking mechanism must have been justified by more than a few Christmas hymns.

Despite the limitations of this instrument, Bach's organ music in the Weimar years surveys a wider range of styles on a bigger scale than had been achieved before by any organist in any European tradition, offering every subsequent composer a model to emulate as best he could. The duke may have 'fired him up' ('feuerte ihn an') but many a court organist strove to please, and in Bach's case there must also have been an extraordinary creative urge, matched by a restless curiosity. The Obituary's remark also serves a purpose: if it came from Bach, it looks like a gracious acknowledgment; but if from the authors, it bears on the poorer support given him later in Leipzig. What is unclear is whether it is speaking of organ music before and after the service – expansive chorales, spectacular toccatas – or items for private ducal concerts. The latter seems unlikely, though it is not out of the question that an exceptional duke would take pleasure in organ music played in his own chapel by a virtuoso employee.

Either way, at Weimar various kinds of organ music were created for playing on various occasions, including perhaps – though this is not certain – after the services. They include toccatas, preludes, fantasias, fugues, perhaps the Passacaglia, improvisations, eventually transcriptions or imitations of solo concertos, as well as exceptional, mixed genres such as a Fugue on the Magnificat, or a Fantasia on the Whit hymn. By now, organ toccatas of the old kind in several sections have become big, subtle, succinct, fully worked concerto-like movements, such as the G major, BWV 541. How often Bach paired a prelude with a particular fugue, either on paper or in performance, is not as certain as supposed by those who now have the *Well-Tempered Clavier* in mind or rely on later editions that do pair them.[1]

Another big question is why the Obituary does not mention harpsichord music or the kinds of chamber music that must have occupied as much time as organ playing. Because more-or-less public organ music was the duke's prime concern? Or because it suited the Obituary's picture of the great organ virtuoso? Or because it was not Bach's duty (nor anyone else's) to compose and play harpsichord music in public? Or indeed because his writing for harpsichord did not develop so magnificently as that for organ until after Weimar? The simplest reason for the virtual silence is that the Obituary authors knew little of any kind of chamber music, including solo harpsichord works: organ music generally remained in use for a longer period, harpsichord styles moved on. So did chamber music, only a few examples of which would survive, and would do so because of being reused in other forms. (So the organ sonatas of c1729 contain several movements that might have originated in Weimar chamber music.) What is at least more certain is that by now Bach was distinguishing 'genuine' organ works from earlier music that equally suited the harpsichord, and surely took as much pleasure in them as the duke did.

The restless curiosity one can confidently attribute to Bach is suggested by other music he knew during his early Weimar years: concertos of Albinoni and Telemann, masses by Peranda and (a little later?) Palestrina, organ and harpsichord works of Grigny and Dieupart, the *St Mark Passion* once attributed to Keiser. The musical quality of these items varies, suggesting that his self-teaching was both serendipitous and discriminating. He came to own copies not only

---

[1] In this connection, it should not be forgotten that the earliest known versions of many *Well-Tempered Clavier* preludes were also separate pieces, not paired with fugues.

of contemporary Thuringian music but of at least three spectacular organ publications originating far from Weimar: Ammerbach's *Tabulaturbuch* (Leipzig, 1571), Frescobaldi's *Fiori musicali* (Venice, 1635) and Grigny's *Livre d'orgue* (Paris, 1699/1700), the last an accurate copy he made himself. While one can trace a few details of such music in Bach's own works, not the least interest he found in these three volumes and others was probably their actual notation, which in each case is quite different from his usual keyboard scores: tablature (Ammerbach), four-stave open score with C clefs (Frescobaldi), three-stave keyboard score with French clefs, intricate ornamentation and a wandering pedal part (Grigny). A dossier could be compiled from Bach's MSS made over a lifetime to suggest that amongst other things his attention was drawn to musical notation itself.

As to traces of Frescobaldi or Grigny in his music: Frescobaldi may prompt much of his mature counterpoint, but nowhere does Bach keep strictly to Grigny's way of writing for the organ. Did he miss the point? Did copying not lead him to grasp the beauty of French solos for the left hand? Or did he think their peculiar lyricism too indulgent for Lutheran chorales or Lutheran organists? At other times, his thoroughness comes close to the pedantic. A mature work such as the Four Duets in *Clavierübung* III systematically includes, but without overstepping the confines of the chosen genre, the various categories of pulse, metre, time signature, mode, key, form, imitation, counterpoint, motif, chromatic, diatonic, etc., as if they were preplanned and ticked off on a list. It is as if an upbringing far from obvious musical centres left him both exceptionally curious and exceptionally determined to master all possibilities, and the penchant to be comprehensive was gradually becoming stronger.

Subtle signs of other composers' influence on him can often be missed. For example, the seven exquisite Advent and Christmas Fughettas are more likely to be prompted by the perfect little fughettas in Frescobaldi's book than by duller work of German organists, just as Frescobaldi's Bergamasca is quite likely to be lurking behind the final Goldberg variation. If these particular Bach works belong to much the same period, c1740, they would imply that the sheer quality of Frescobaldi's book remained impressed on him for decades after he acquired a copy at Weimar in 1714 – and justifiably so. Were he to have been still voicing admiration for Frescobaldi during the 1740s one can more easily understand why Emanuel came to single him out when naming influences in the Obituary.

The Weimar years found Bach still composing chorales in the 'local' way, separating the verse lines with interludes, or giving the melody in canon, or planning a big fantasia in several paragraphs. The strongest drive in all his maturing work, whatever the genre, is without doubt his mastery of invertible counterpoint, a manner of composing in which either of two lines can serve as the lower and which, when handled by a master, generates virtually any kind of music. It held no fears for J. S. Bach and led to a huge and totally unmatched array of works, from Weimar cantata movements to the later organ sonatas, from chorales to the later Inventions, from a Mühlhausen cantata to the B minor Mass. Simpler hymn variations, usually miscalled chorale partitas, barely survived into the Weimar period, and one can understand why. In 1802, Forkel claimed that Bach found writing variations a 'thankless task' (p. 52), because of their reiterated harmony. Perhaps Emanuel or Friedemann said so, or Forkel assumed it from the rarity of variation sets in the Bach oeuvre, by comparison with Handel's or Mozart's. It seems to be true, and one notes that four outstanding, indeed unique variation works – Cantata 4, the organ Passacaglia, the violin Chaconne, the harpsichord Goldberg – do everything but reiterate the harmony in some simple way.

For its picture of the serious composer, the Obituary described the Weimar job in terms of organ music and, after Bach was promoted to concertmeister, 'mainly church pieces'. The realm of concert music is ignored, and yet, as subsequent researches have made clear, of monumental importance to the composer, something conceivably changing his musical life for ever, was his (sudden?) acquaintance in 1713 with the new Venetian concertos.

When the young Prince Johann Ernst returned from Holland with copies of Vivaldi and other Italians, probably including Corelli, it was sets of playing parts he sent in his luggage, and there is every reason to suppose that his teacher Walther and the court keyboardist Bach soon had them on their music desks, ready to play. Not only were concertos arranged by Bach for organ or harpsichord – scored up from the parts, one might say – but it is hard to imagine at least some of the Brandenburgs and later solo concertos existing without the revelations offered by, say, Vivaldi's Op. 3, which has a dashing quality beyond even Corelli. Vivaldi shows how to organise long 'abstract' pieces by means of judicious repetition, inventive note-spinning and simple harmony handled with such rhythmic vitality as to excite the listener in a new way. Walther, who had shared Bach's interest in both French music and Palestrina masses (BJ 2002, p. 17), also arranged many Venetian concertos, probably at a period when the young prince was composing his own works in this style under Walther's tutelage. Telemann got to hear of his efforts and published some, and Bach arranged others, making from one in G major a version for organ and a version for harpsichord.

To give a piece of music length, to sustain a movement and allow it to develop and come to a well-paced conclusion, continued to be of great interest to Bach, as did the 'perfect miniature' whose brevity meant all was said that need be. The result at Weimar was on the one hand the succinct nine-bar prelude of the *Orgelbüchlein* and on the other the expansive movements in cantatas and concertos. Samuel Johnson's remark that Milton could create a colossus but not carve a head upon a cherry stone would not apply to J. S. Bach. His success on both the small and the large scale results from merging melodic flair with real harmonic tension, and of the two, the second is paramount. Lines that are themselves melodious also create logical harmony, and there is an uncanny grasp of how a simple common chord can be as beautiful as a complex discord, and vice versa. Seldom does harmonic grasp fail him, though it can, as at one moment in the Fugue in F major BWV 540.

Usually, if a movement strikes one as not very inspired (some arias in Cantata 12?), it is hard to discern the problem: melody or harmony or both? Keyboard works in which at some point he places a theme upside down can arouse curiosity, even a smile, but the harmony or the melodic line itself sometimes suffers. In the case of cantata movements, too much attention paid to picturing a text in the music can lead to a prosaic quality in the melody and harmony, especially when a convention is automatically applied – as in using chromatic intervals for something anxious, sad, regretful or otherwise negative.

Chromatic motifs are an example of a time-honoured means of composing with *figurae* – little note patterns giving impetus to a coherent harmony – and one much practised by Walther and Bach during this period. Walther actually outlined many of the *figurae* in an unpublished treatise written for Prince Johann Ernst, the *Praecepta* of 1708, and Bach produced a wide range of works constructed on this principle. One could view the unique and astonishingly beautiful 'Little Organ Book' (*Orgelbüchlein*) as the peak of this tradition, for its melodies are harmonised in such a way and with such note patterns as would establish a mood for the text, even *picture* it. At times, one has the impression that in this practical book Bach is realising, at a level of unheard-of sophistication, the very details outlined by his colleague Walther in his theoretical book. The two men were surely aware of each other's activities, even forming an active network with their respective students. Did they discuss such techniques, perhaps vying with each other? Walther's own music often uses the very patterns handled with incomparable inventiveness by Bach, and a case can certainly be made that they were competing to create good canons from certain hymn tunes.

The local tactics of using little note patterns needs an overall strategy for creating shape and length. In the *Orgelbüchlein*, or a cantata movement based on a chorale, there is no problem, since the chorale melody gives the form. But what of a substantial piece of music without such props? How correct one is to see Vivaldi's concertos as helping Bach shape the movements of his own concertos – which, like the big organ preludes and fugues, are lone works anticipated by no predecessor and matched by no successor – is not obvious. For he had long been writing fugues which tend by nature towards a kind of concerto form, in which the 'subject' returns regularly after 'episodes', which vary in key, length, texture or scoring and thus introduce both variety and repetition.

Although the sustained endeavour evident in a Bach work, its avoidance of easy or lazy ways of proceeding, might have metamorphosed into the great structures without his ever knowing a single Venetian concerto, in fact the Italian conception does seem to have been an inspiration for his systematic treatment. Types of theme, rhythm and reiterated chords can be recognised as Italian in inspiration, though sustained longer than they might be in Vivaldi's Op. 3 or Op. 7. In the dance movements of the (later) English Suites for harpsichord, one sees a comparable stretching of convention, in this case of French idioms picked up from suites by Dieupart or d'Anglebert, or even from Couperin's *Premier livre* of 1713. The English Suites are a good instance of Bach's careful adopting of styles, for although on one level they are impeccable – well-wrought preludes, courantes with model syncopations, sarabandes with model harmonies, etc. – they lack the caprice and 'thoughtless' panache of Parisian composers. They try so hard, too hard, working their counterpoint so thoroughly that a player can sometimes find them less pleasurable, even less idiomatic to the harpsichord, than relatively brainless pieces by French composers.

Apparent contradictions in Bach's music, at Weimar and throughout his life, give some idea of his inner musical life. One such contradiction is that the very completeness of his coverage – his tendency to 'tick off a list' of parameters – was no barrier to achieving quality or even, one might say, fun. For example, he may have deliberately planned the organ toccata in C major to show off different ways of optionally using two manuals, to which not every player of the time had access, doing so with a real sense of play. The first movement uses them antiphonally (two themes, two manuals) and for echoes (opening solo); the second as a melody plus accompaniment; the third for subject and episodes in a long fugue. This could result in a mere didactic demonstration but does not, so easily transcending the didactic with great verve and melody that no copyists, and very few players today, seem to be aware that it can be interpreted in this way.

A second contradiction in Bach is even more elusive: the sensuality of his music at moments of marked piety, in arias or in the *Orgelbüchlein*. The harmony is often so new and rich that one can only assume his piety allowed for, even embraced, the intense pleasure given him by his sense of hearing. In the two arias of Cantata 115, a Leipzig work, the *Affekt* of penitence is calculated and explicit, and yet the first aria's rich texture and the second aria's minor-ninth chords are so sensuously rich as to seem well beyond the call of mere piety. Other, different examples are the opening bars of the third and sixth Brandenburg, where the pulsating chords please and excite; Cantata 182, where the opening melody is pure delight; and Cantata 54, like No. 182 a Weimar work, which begins unexpectedly on a rich, throbbing discord. This discord, which takes time to resolve, is assumed to be alluding to the text's command to 'resist sins', but the allusion would be nothing without the chord's powerful beauty. In fact, not for the first time this beauty raises a question about music's powers of allusion: is one resisting sin with a resistant discord or is the discord sinfully resisting resolution? If the latter, is it aiming to show sin as something attractive that we do not want to resist (resolve)?

These and other effects are creations of a man responding to the sense-enchantment of good harmony and able to make it behave in ways unknown again before the middle of the nineteenth century. Even in the late *Art of Fugue* one can still experience the sheer pleasure of harmony on a well-tuned keyboard despite the intricacy of its immensely skilful four-part counterpoint. The sensual side of Bach's personality cannot have been exclusive to music, and one wonders how he dealt with it in daily life. Was it no problem for him to achieve both the cerebral and the sensuous? In his personal life, did he always achieve equilibrium between the two?

[In 1713] after the death of Zachow, music director and organist at the Market Church in Halle [on 7 August 1712], Bach received a call to take the position there. He did indeed go to Halle and performed his trial work there. But he found reasons to reject this position, which [Gottfried] Kirchhof then took.

It is curious that Zachow is mentioned by name when, in the account of the Leipzig position ten years later, Bach's predecessor there (Kuhnau) is not. Was it because Zachow, though not on Emanuel's list of composers his father admired, was widely known as the teacher of Handel, who had visited Halle during the previous winter (HHB, p. 57)? Perhaps Handel was the preferred if unlikely candidate to succeed him, and known to be so? And perhaps Kirchhof is mentioned as successor because *his* eventual successor in 1746 was Friedemann? Whatever is the case, turning down jobs was not a thing to keep quiet about, especially since the job searches by big parish churches were such public events. Walther's *Lexicon* of 1732 had also reported Kirchhof as declining invitations to become capellmeister in two princely courts, positions which, being privately filled, would have been less widely known about.

Two big questions are whether Bach did apply in the normal way at the Market Church (Liebfrauenkirche), and why in any case he declined. Very likely he was an adviser for the building of its fine new and large three-manual organ of sixty-five stops, contracted for a month or so after Zachow died. And he became an eventual examiner of it in 1716, with Kuhnau and Kirchhof. His two-week stay there over November–December 1713 seems rather long just to make an interim inspection of the organ, however, so perhaps he was indeed asked to apply for the vacancy, which he then explored fully and formally by composing and performing a cantata as requested by the chief pastor J. M. Heineccius. That the church paid for both the cantata and his hotel stay could mean that he was treated (i.e. asked to be treated) as a guest, and he claimed later not to have actually applied for the job, only to have 'presented himself' ('um die Stelle angehalten mich praesentiret': *Dok* I, pp. 23–4). A distinction was evidently intended between the two, again like those people today who speak of being 'head-hunted'. Bach's words, written in March 1714, were part of what looks like a tetchy reply to an accusation made by the people at Halle that he had 'played such a trick' ('solche tour gespielet') in order to solicit more money for his position in Weimar.

What is clear is that Bach was offered the Halle job, was thought to have accepted it there and then (Dok II, p. 49), and was sent a draft contract in mid-December; that he delayed a month and then declined, saying he had not yet received 'complete dismissal' from Weimar ('völlige dimission': Dok I, p. 21), and asking for changes to be made to the salary (an increase) and duties (a reduction); that he said he would reply in full when current work at Weimar allowed (surely this was stalling?); and that then, probably in February 1714, he withdrew completely. This was a week or two before the confirmation that he was promoted to concertmeister at Weimar, with a salary increase, a promotion he had requested (Dok II, p. 53). The Halle people must have learnt of this and accused him of playing tricks, but in reply he asks why he should relocate even at the same salary, let alone a lower one, and particularly before entitlement to other fees in the Halle church had been clarified. The story is surely not to his credit, however. There is tetchiness in saying that he had no need to travel to Halle for the duke to raise his salary, pride in claiming not actually to have applied for the job, and disingenuousness in saying that a learned lawyer such as his Halle correspondent could judge whether he was right not to change jobs for the same salary.

And yet, no doubt Bach was valued in Weimar, and it could be that the frequency with which money and pay crop up in connection with him is a misleading consequence of his now being represented chiefly by formal documents. The facts that he was apparently well received in Halle at the organ test of 1716 and had by then set a text by the Halle minister to the music of Cantata 63 suggest that by no means did he become non grata. Perhaps the board, genuinely disappointed, knew their offer was not good enough and were avoiding blame. Besides, even creative musicians need to be practical.[2] Sebastian's elder brother Christoph did not take over Pachelbel's position at Gotha when his salary at Ohrdruf was increased, nor, for a similar reason in 1759, did Sebastian's son Johann Christoph Friedrich leave Bückeburg for Altona, Hamburg.

Nevertheless, it is clear that Bach was not backward in establishing himself financially as well as possible. One wonders whether, when earlier at Weimar his employer raised his salary because his deceased predecessor Effler no longer needed a pension, Bach had actually solicited on these grounds, and if so, why there was no mention of Effler's widow (NBR, p. 60). His own widow in Leipzig was to live on modest pensions from church, city and university.

The Halle incident raises a question about the book of chorales called 'Orgelbüchlein', important in view of its special qualities. If its earliest entries are correctly dated to Advent 1713, perhaps it was begun not for services and/or pupils at Weimar but as a chorale book for Halle, suiting that church's Pietist notions of worship and hymn singing. 'Orgelbüchlein' was a title more appropriate when added eight or nine years later, when young Friedemann had probably begun studying the *Well-Tempered Clavier*. Originally, the collection could have started as a response to the kind of Pietist Lutheranism of which Halle became a well-known centre: a personalised, introspective religious practice which emphasised crushing contrition and a biting conscience that leaves the believer assured of grace. Music supporting such beliefs would appeal directly to personal feelings, aiming to elicit emotional response rather than teach doctrine.

The *Orgelbüchlein* chorales are unusually simple in concept and meet the stipulations of the Halle contract, which were as follows (Dok II, p. 50):

---

[2] Handel, not a family man, risked his 1,000-thaler-a-year position in Hanover when he overstayed his leave in London in 1713.

Bach was to accompany the chorales chosen by the minister 'slowly' and
  'without special decoration' ('langsam ohne sonderbahres coloriren')
  in four or five parts (so their harmony was neither too thin nor too thick)
  drawing the organ's basic 8′ stops (Principal, Quintaden, Gedackt, reeds)
  and changing them in each verse
realising the harmony with syncopations and suspensions in such a way that
  the congregation feels supported by the harmony.

'Accompany' could mean not (or not only) playing while the congregation sang the hymn but introducing it, perhaps interspersing its verses
with interludes, giving the people a music clearly matching the sentiments of the text. Perhaps in some apprehension of the large new
organ then being built, the authorities wanted all this done by using
the organ in a discreet and varied, non-monotonous manner.

Although the Halle clerk was not quite confident with technical
language, his meaning is clear and could help to explain how it comes
about that the Orgelbüchlein is so different from the usual collections of
chorales – richer, shorter, distinctive, 'warmer' in Affekt. When in 1746
Bach's ex-pupil J. G. Ziegler applied at the same church for the job that
went to W. F. Bach, he specifically said that his teacher had instructed
him to play the hymns not indifferently but according to the Affekt of
the words (Dok II, p. 423), something that the church's ministers would
have traditionally desired. Moreover, appropriate hymn playing 'with
beautiful harmony' had also been specified at Halle in 1702, when the
seventeen-year-old Handel was appointed organist in the city's modest
cathedral (HHB, p. 18). Such care seems typical of a community known
for its devotional approach to all forms of religious observance.

Bach began a massive collection of 164 chorales, more than ever at-
tempted before, so far as is known, but he completed a little more than
a quarter and then called a halt. Why? Perhaps new duties at Weimar
in March 1714 (see below) meant that an assistant now played for the
hymns and/or Bach now preferred making longer chorales, having less
need than in Halle for settings of such a succinct, melodious kind. The
later additions to the book seem to be attempts by an orderly-minded
composer to complete what he had begun, irrespective of changed

circumstances or perhaps for the sake of eventual but unrealised publication. Had Bach gone to Halle, not only is the book of chorales more likely to have been finished but one can speculate on how his cantatas could have been more 'approachable', more immediately 'affecting', less 'doctrinal' than those for Leipzig.

The situation at Weimar was different in many respects from Halle, not least the actual hymn singing. Its hymns were led by a group of eight choirboys located in a gallery behind the altar, much nearer to the court personnel on the chapel floor or first gallery than the organ was. A practical question concerns any chorale played at Weimar by its organ high and distant in a ceiling gallery: is one to imagine first a prelude wafting down from on high, then the choristers singing, then a court congregation joining in, with the verses separated by organ interludes?

In 1714 [2 March] he was named concertmeister at the same court. However, at that time the functions connected with this position consisted mainly in having to compose church pieces and perform them.

The force of 'however' is that a concertmeister would not normally be the person writing cantatas for the court's chapel, and that direction of the concert or theatre music such as it was remained in the hands of the capellmeister. The phrase 'and perform them' seems to be there to make it clear that it was Bach who directed these cantatas, not the capellmeister; and perhaps one is also to infer that he negotiated this specially. In addition, he continued to be court organist (Dok II, p. 63)[3] and probably harpsichordist in chamber music, and within a year was being paid the same as the capellmeister (Dok II, p. 57).

How much call Bach still had for writing organ chorales is not known, but his position in the particular world of organs was locally unrivalled, attracting attention from both prospective students and organ committees. When engaged as organ examiner (Mühlhausen 1709 (?),

---

[3] As in a collegiate chapel today, this would not necessarily mean playing the hymns.

Taubach 1710, Halle 1716, Erfurt Augustinerkirche 1716, Leipzig university church 1717) it is likely that he played a public concert of his grander works, such as the toccatas in C major and D minor, or various preludes and fugues in G major and C major, and indeed chorale settings. Many of the bigger pieces existed in several versions, no doubt many more than are now known about, and a likely reason why their dating and purpose are such guesswork is that they were portfolio works selected and revised as the occasion required. The idea of one authoritative version of works such as this, and indeed of a composer's oeuvre as a whole, is rather modern.

The cantatas or 'new pieces to be performed monthly' that were expected of Bach following promotion at Weimar (Dok II, p. 53) were ensemble works of several movements sung after the creed and before the seasonal hymn and sermon. Capellmeister Drese was responsible for the other weeks, and one can imagine Bach agitating for this monthly commission and the authority to direct it. How far the promotion was a reason to decline the Halle position is questionable, since there he would have had similar or better opportunities, but perhaps performance standards and the aristocratic context at Weimar were an attraction. For Bach brought to the ducal chapel subtle, chamber-like works of refined forces (four singers, a five-part instrumental consort), with newly created effects and colourful timbres, varying and unpredictable sequences of instrumental and vocal movements, with texts drawn from the newest devotional libretti. These last included some by Salomo Franck, Weimar court secretary and librarian, and Erdmann Neumeister, soon to become chief pastor of the Jakobikirche, Hamburg, the scene of another job opportunity for Bach, in 1720. The cantatas that resulted at Weimar were far from the usual 'parish church music', works which he must have spent a lot of time and effort polishing.

In the Bach cantata as it was emerging, fully fledged movements rather than mere sections would contrast with each other as they set, in a sequence, various texts drawn from Old or New Testament, from newly written poetry, and from the corpus of chorale texts familiar to Lutheran congregations. Cantatas dating from after the 1714 promotion have an opening chorus (from Palm Sunday to Christmas, 1714), mostly after an instrumental introduction. Typical is a counterpoint based on the permutation principle, in which themes have countersubjects always accompanying them but in different vertical orders, giving a concentrated and 'systematic' impression to the sound.

Although a salary increase in June 1713 implies that Bach had sometimes provided cantatas already in Weimar (Nos. 18, 199, perhaps 208), the first cantata performed under the new dispensation was No. 182, whose opening sonata leads off with a charming violin theme (played by the composer?), elegantly setting the new tone: a cantata uniting disparate movements, including chamber choruses, recitative, a sequence of arias, a chorale and finally a choral dance rather like a passepied. Even when the cantatas from 1715 or 1716 (e.g. Nos. 161–163, 185) restricted the chorus to a final chorale – in principle, rather like finales in the standard Italian opera – their chamber scoring creates a quite different effect from that of the chorales closing the later Leipzig cantatas. These have a more 'congregational' feel to them such as suits a large parish church, whether or not the congregation actually joined in singing them.

Some eighteen cantatas for the period 1713–17 exist and another five are documented, leaving open some questions – not only where are the other twenty or so from three and a half years of monthly and occasional cantatas, but also how do the eighteen come to survive at all? Those two questions are related and imply that what survives of any ensemble works (belonging not to a composer but to his employer) depends on circumstances. If in 1717 Bach did write no cantatas, was it pique at not automatically having succeeded the deceased capellmeister Drese Sr the previous December? Or perhaps he had sometimes performed pieces by other composers, even by Drese Jr, who had been in Venice and must have learnt something about recitatives and ABA arias, and for all we know was a thorn in concertmeister Bach's flesh. Special cantatas, as for Christmas (No. 63) or Easter (No. 31), would be scored for bigger ensembles, choral or instrumental, while cantatas for obscurer occasions (No. 54) were scored for smaller.

The cantatas vary in shape, probably reflecting local tradition rather than Italian imports, and seem consciously to survey all conceivable kinds of music possible within a specific genre – a typical Bach characteristic. One never knows quite what kind of melody or texture or scoring or shape or movement type is to come next. (A similar point could be made about Handel's concerti grossi.) But how touching or moving a court congregation would find the decorated chorale closing No. 161 or the picturesque door-knocking in No. 61 is hard to know. They look like the effects of a clever rather than a stirring composer. What is clearer is that having begun his Advent cantata No. 61 with a French *ouverture*, appropriate for the opening of the church year, Bach could begin another Advent cantata (No. 62) ten years later by basing it on the same melody but now in the manner of an Italian concerto, equally polished but different in all respects. Such systematic coverage of the possibilities was a lifelong aim.

The concertmeister's duties could well have included violin playing, perhaps as leader. How subservient Bach was to the capellmeister and vice-capellmeister is not known, though a ducal directive in March 1714 that rehearsals must now take place in the chapel might have been instigated by Bach himself, to have them on neutral territory and so more under his control. (Who now was the thorn in the flesh?) He was also responsible for the big festive cantata No. 208, performed on commission for the birthday celebrations of the Duke of Saxe-Weissenfels in February 1713 and perhaps at other times.

Cantata 208 is a major work with elements both old (charming short-phrased melodies) and new (recitatives, horn solos), striving to develop the topics of hunting and *pastorella* according to conventions of the day, perhaps over-thoughtfully but still melodiously. Its plan resembles an opera act with a series of arias in da capo (ABA) or concerto (ritornello) form, and seems to lead naturally towards Brandenburg Concerto No. 1. This last may be either a compilation whose first movement originally prefaced Cantata No. 208, or a full concerto from the Weimar period later revised in order to open the Marquis of Brandenburg's set of six (see below, p. 81). In exploring special instrumental combinations, the Brandenburgs match the Weimar cantatas, although the leisurely paced harmonies of the third and sixth concerto are more mature, resulting from contemplating Vivaldi's string idioms. On the composer's title page, the French word 'concert' implies not 'concerto' in a modern sense but what the English meant by 'consort music', pieces in several movements to be played by one or other combination of instruments, amateur or professional.

Bach did not automatically become capellmeister on Drese Sr's death in December 1716, despite writing cantatas for that period (Advent) and hoping, one supposes, to be preferred above Drese Jr. When no appointment was made, his interest in Weimar could well have waned, hence the blank months of 1717. Other possibilities are that the chapel music deteriorated in the interregnum, and/or that Bach was more or less silenced for a year by the senior duke for his loyalty to the junior. The two dukes' constant contention certainly exposed the distasteful side of a court run on absolutist lines. But whatever the case, Bach's creativity would have had no trouble in turning more to instrumental and keyboard music were he to have sought a different position elsewhere.

> In Weimar he also trained not a few fine organists.

Adding to the picture of Bach's active musical life at Weimar as outlined by the Obituary – organ playing, composing cantatas and organ music, participating in chamber music, teaching – sources give a glimpse of a dozen or so pupils. Extant MSS show his keyboard works being copied by such gifted pupils as J. T. Krebs and J. C. Vogler, though for what purpose can only be surmised: models of composition, or repertory for the present and future? J. G. Walther would make several copies of the same piece, perhaps (like a contemporary of his, the London organist John Reading) to keep at different locations. Although Bach's pupils are often now listed in such numbers as to imply that he had a brilliant reputation as a teacher, it is unclear how exceptional the numbers were or how unusual were the abilities of a few of them. His students' warm praise for their teacher in job applications does not give a sure picture, any more than it would today.

Nevertheless, pupils using a teacher's name to support their own *bona fides* do reveal a little. Hence Ziegler's reference to being taught by Bach to play chorales according to their sentiment (see above, p. 62) is particularly relevant to Halle. P. D. Kräuter's request in 1711–13 to his school board at home, who were sponsoring his study, gives several useful pieces of information about the situation in Weimar (Dok III, pp. 649–50). Thus, it seems he travelled all the way from Augsburg to Weimar for lessons with the court organist – clearly, there was nothing exceptional in the young Bach having gone as far as Lübeck. As with Buxtehude, any fame Bach had would not be 'as a composer' or 'as an organist' but simply as 'the famous musician', even though still aged only twenty-six. Whether by 1711 any of Bach's compositions had penetrated to Augsburg is not documented, though by 1717 Mattheson in Hamburg reports in print that he has seen both choral and keyboard works of his (Dok II, p. 65), and Kräuter doubtless took some back when he returned to take up a position in Augsburg in 1713.

For a year's lessons plus board and lodging, presumably in his own house, Bach asked a hundred thaler which Kräuter got lowered to eighty or, for the sake of his sponsors, said he did. As to the instruction itself, the pupil received six hours a day of 'guidance' ('zur Information'), in composition, *Clavier* and other instruments. Perhaps 'six hours' was also to impress the Augsburg sponsors. It probably included copying parts for his teacher, though none of them seem to have survived. He was also free to look through his master's work, a detail which confirms the right of a fee-paying pupil to use and copy his teacher's work, and which indirectly sheds some light on the moonlight anecdote. The general picture is one of serious sustained study, comparable to a professional college today if its curriculum were ever to be pared down to crucial, core study. In 1732, the father of C. H. Gräbner of Dresden, one of Bach's Leipzig pupils, in remarking that his son's lessons with Bach in Leipzig had cost him 'not a little' (Dok II, p. 228), clearly saw them

* **Jch habe von dem berühmtenOrganiften zuWei=
mar/ Hrn. Joh. Sebaftian Bach/ Sachen ge=
fehen/ fo wohl vor die Kirche als vor die Fauft/
die gewiß fo befchaffen find/ daß man den Mann
hoch æftimiren muß. Db diefer Bach einer
von des oberwehnten Johann Michel Bachs
Nachfommen ift/ davon habe feine rechteKund=
fchafft/und will ihn hiemit erfuchen/zum Behueff
des in der Dedication gegenwärtigen Wercks
erwehnten Vorhabens/ wo müglich/ behülfflich
zu feyn.**

3 First reference in print to J. S. Bach.

From Johannes Mattheson, *Das beschützte Orchestre* (Hamburg, 1717), p. 222.

Translation: 'I have seen things by the famous organist in Weimar, Mr Joh. Sebastian Bach, both for the church [i.e. cantatas] as for the fist [i.e. keyboard music] that are certainly made in such a way that one must esteem the man highly. Whether this Bach is a descendant of Johann Michael Bach mentioned above [his father-in-law] I have no reliable information and want hereby to ask him to be as helpful as he can with respect to the plan mentioned in the dedication of the present work.' This plan was to compile a biographical dictionary.

as a key qualification for his son in seeking an important position in Dresden.

Lessons as we know them today but lasting six hours are unlikely: rather, Kräuter's day-long contact was as an apprentice to a master, observing and being useful, accompanying him in his duties, hearing or participating in music including newly imported works, learning how to compose Italian and French instrumental music, getting to know an organ's structure (and costs) from the work under way in the Weimar chapel, and altogether 'seeing, hearing and copying a great deal' ('vil sehen, hören und decopirt'). At much the same period as Kräuter but in London, Maurice Greene was similarly articled to the organist of St Paul's and eventually succeeded him, as Bach's pupil J. M. Schubart succeeded him at Weimar. As the Obituary makes clear, though whether with pride is not entirely clear, Bach himself had not been regularly articled as a pupil to a master in this way.

With respect to musical training, Bach's own children may have been treated similarly to live-in pupils, who also included family cousins. And as with the seventy-odd pupils documented from the Leipzig years, some of them would have been regular copyists for the performing parts of their master's cantatas and instrumental works, extracted from his fair-copy score. One cousin, Johann Elias, became tutor for younger Bach children in Leipzig in 1737–42 and secretary to their father, as other pupils probably did. This Elias is notable for some surviving letters in which he gives a few details of life in the household twenty years or more after Weimar – pitifully few details, though from them we do learn that Anna Magdalena was a keen gardener and Sebastian had a sweet tooth, liking cider as well as (so other references say) beer, brandy, coffee and tobacco.

Although they need not have had the elevated title 'secretary' or 'treasurer', as J. C. Schmidt Sr had with Handel in London, no doubt other young relations and/or pupils of Bach served as some kind of personal assistant living in the house. Emanuel is speaking of the Leipzig years when he called the busy family house a dovecot ('Taubenhaus': Dok III, p. 290), with people coming in and out all the time, his father too busy to engage in correspondence. But the Weimar situation cannot have been so very different, except that presumably there were fewer distinguished visitors. 'Too busy for correspondence' could be an oblique reference to the kind of open letters on musical *arcana* apparently written by Handel, Krieger and others, regularly published by Mattheson in his *Critica musica*, a publication which never numbered J. S. Bach amongst its contributors. Another late witness spoke of concerts in the Bach house in Leipzig, at which father and sons played, and one can suppose the situation in Weimar to have been similar, with musical gatherings involving pupils, court colleagues and a precocious young Friedemann.

Why the Obituary mentions organist-pupils specifically at Weimar when there must have been six times as many in Leipzig is unclear – to establish the authority Bach already had in his twenties? Or perhaps in Leipzig instruction for occasional pupils, university students and, as time passed, visiting admirers was less on the organ and more in music generally? (And considering church organs needed bellows blowers, were 'organ lessons' mostly on practice instruments, blown by whoever was available?) J. P. Kirnberger, adopting the mantle of fugue expert after Bach's death, wrote about studying fugues in such lessons, while another pupil, H. N. Gerber, spoke of learning to play them (*Dok* III, pp. 362, 476). Instruction in Weimar cannot have been very different. If it was there that he began to prepare for the *Well-Tempered Clavier*, it could have been in response to such recent publications as J. K. F. Fischer's fifteen preludes and fugues (reissued in 1715) and J. H. Buttstedt's treatise discussing fugal answers (Erfurt, 1716). The *WTC* looks very much like a deliberate attempt to surpass other instructional collections by developing fully fledged preludes and fugues, varied beyond anyone's previous imagination.

An important amount of keyboard music must belong to the Weimar period, studied by pupils or played in chamber concerts or preserved for private use, as the case may be. By no means are the harpsichord transcriptions of Italian and other concertos BWV 972–987 of minor interest, showing as they do the influence of the string music newly imported in the years around 1715, and teaching how to shape instrumental movements without the text of cantatas and motets or the small-scale set forms of dances and variations. These transcriptions offer a range of new melodies and movement shapes, new keyboard effects and layouts, comparing well with the more local produce and giving the player now, as they must have given Bach, a welcome breath of fresh air after the turgidity of the earlier Reinken transcriptions.

And yet, several of Bach's transcriptions for organ and harpsichord suggest that he either did not understand the natural verve and rhetoric of Venetian string concertos or else wished to temper it with German 'seriousness'. It is otherwise difficult to know why, when he came to transcribe them for keyboard, he filled in the perfectly effective rests often found in Vivaldi's string concertos with bits of busy counterpoint – even, in the case of the concerto BWV 593, cleverly deriving these bits of counterpoint from one of Vivaldi's own themes.

There are not a few instances of such otioseness. Similarly, it has been customary to attribute to the work on these concertos Bach's grasp of long-breathed structures, in which main themes return regularly enough to create a sense of organicism without tiresome repetition. But a key difference is that Italian concerto forms are often loose and capricious, deliberately asymmetrical, while many of Bach's are the opposite, long and thorough, giving an impression of being exhaustive. Such movements can do this even when, as in the six sonatas for organ, they are petite and almost miniature. His harpsichord and violin concertos have long movements carefully planned around various keys, contrapuntal in detail, breaking off a returning theme in order to shoot off in another direction, and resulting in a 'thoroughness' that becomes typical of all kinds of pieces. Each movement of the Chromatic Fantasia and Fugue, a quite spectacular work, shows in its own distinctive way wonderfully sustained paragraphs and an overall shape far beyond anything achieved in the preludes or fugues of any predecessor. But the first movement works hard for its *fantasy*, and the second is quite without it.

> The year 1717 gave a new opportunity to our Bach, already so famous, to achieve still more honour: Marchand, the harpsichordist and organist famous in France, had come to Dresden . . . [concertmeister Volumier] created an opportunity for Bach to hear his opponent first in secret. Bach invited him courteously by hand to a contest . . . Marchand showed himself very willing [but on the date appointed,] to the greatest astonishment, it was learnt that very early on the same day Monsieur Marchand had departed Dresden by special coach.

Unfortunately, this, the biggest single biographical item in the Obituary – twice as long as the moonlight anecdote – tells us little about the composer, neither whether he was a fine interpreter of Marchand's suites, as was said later (*Dok* III, p. 125), nor even whether he was reluctant to talk about the competition, as was said later still (*Dok* III,

p. 443). The latter is doubtful, for the differing details in the story as variously reported look like the result of a middle-aged man's retelling of an old anecdote.

Emanuel probably knew that the first reference in print to his father was dated 1717 and so realised he was indeed 'already so famous', as the Obituary says. Or he could assume it from an account of the Dresden competition published by J. A. Birnbaum in 1739. Birnbaum, Bach's defender against some recent criticisms (see below, p. 168), had presumably learnt about it from the composer himself, whom the criticisms probably goaded into publicising his achievements and claims to fame. Again, therefore, it looks as if the Obituary was taking up something that had already been published, the more particularly as, not long before, Mattheson had told of another, earlier Dresden contest, between the 'local' man Matthias Weckmann and another distinguished visitor, J. J. Froberger (1740, p. 396). Also, from yet another printed account (Titon Du Tillet's *Parnasse*, 1732), well-read musicians anywhere might know that Louis Marchand was considered by some to have been the best French keyboardist of his day, more gifted than Couperin or Rameau. Whether or not Emanuel knew it, Marchand was also the composer of a piece in Anna Magdalena's album, now attributed to Couperin who published it. Altogether, then, a story of Bach conquering Marchand was by no means pointless, comparable in fact to Handel instructing Corelli as recounted by Mainwaring a few years later.

The salient points of a story probably not unique in the days of competitions between professionals, seem to be these:

The Dresden concertmeister Volumier invited Bach to meet with Louis Marchand, who had been offered a position with a large salary at the court of Saxony.

Bach heard Marchand play (according to the Obituary, but not Birnbaum) and expressed admiration for his playing (ditto).

He wrote to him (in French?) suggesting an extemporisation contest; Marchand agreed.

The contest was to take place in a court official's house, with the elector's knowledge.

Many people (of both sexes) waited expectantly but discovered Marchand had
   left early that morning.
The elector's reward to Bach was misappropriated by a servant.

Why the Obituary says the listeners were 'of both sexes' is unclear:
because the electress, also a potential employer, was there too and had
a vested interest in Marchand being victorious, hoping he would settle
in Dresden? No French sources give the story, but a Dresden document
shows Marchand receiving payment in the autumn of 1717 (BJ 1998,
p. 14).
   Several other conjectures can be made about the episode:

It cannot have been before October, shortly after the elector returned from
   Italy.
Since J. D. Heinichen was court capellmeister, perhaps Marchand was to
   direct the (Roman Catholic) chapel, or the electress's music.
The contest centred on harpsichord and chamber music. Perhaps the fifth
   Brandenburg Concerto was first drafted for the occasion, with Dresden's
   musical 'specialities' in mind (harpsichord, transverse flute, virtuoso
   violin). Its slow movement seems to use a theme by Marchand (Pirro 1907,
   p. 429).

Until Gottfried Silbermann built his first organ in Dresden, in the
Sophienkirche in 1718–20, there was probably no fine organ available
for a competition, so spectacular music for harpsichord, 'in a court
official's house', was more appropriate. Other possibilities are that
Bach offered harpsichord or that Marchand demanded it, since German
organs were too different from what he was used to.
   Two final conjectures concern possible job applications:

Though Bach, anxious to leave Weimar, was committed to Cöthen (see below),
   the possibility of an incomparably better job in Dresden crossed his mind.
Two years later, Handel too was in Dresden, according to the Count Flemming
   (HHB, p. 83) in whose house Forkel claimed the Bach–Marchand contest
   was to have taken place (1802, p. 8). Was Handel also there for a job – to
   succeed Lotti as royal opera composer? Was Flemming contriving to get
   both Bach and Handel to be in Dresden?

Perhaps the visits to Dresden and, earlier that year, Gotha (Good Friday 1717) were part of a search for a good court appointment at a time when Bach saw he was not to become capellmeister in Weimar. How or even whether he knew Volumier previously is not documented, and by the time of the Obituary every single significant personage involved had died. But it is entirely characteristic of an anecdote J. S. Bach himself might have told that it should include something about lost money: sympathy is being solicited over a reward (if it ever existed) going astray.

The reference to Bach made in print by Mattheson in 1717 includes a request for further biographical information, a request repeated in 1719, on each occasion apparently without answer (Dok II, pp. 65, 75).

4 Cöthen, 1717–1723

In this very same year [1717] . . . the then Prince Leopold of
Anhalt-Cöthen, a great connoisseur and lover of music, called
him to be his capellmeister. He took up the position straightway
and held it for almost six years, to the greatest satisfaction of his
gracious prince.

The Obituary says that Bach entered the prince's service immediately on
returning from the abortive Dresden competition. If Emanuel is right
(see further below), the competition must have been in December,
because in Weimar from 6 November to 2 December 1717 his father
was in prison, held in the 'district judge's cell . . . on account of his
show of obstinacy and for overpressing his dismissal' ('halßstarrigen
Bezeugung und zu erzwingenden dimission: Dok II, p. 65), being finally
released only in disgrace. The Obituary, of course, says nothing about
this.

The duke seems to have had a double complaint against Bach, obstinacy and importunity, but neither is quite clear now. Had he been remon-
strating against J. W. Drese Jr recently succeeding as capellmeister,
after Telemann had declined the position?[1] Or did Drese Jr succeed

---

[1] So Telemann later said (Mattheson 1740, p. 364). It is likely that the Obituary
   authors knew this claim – it was in print – and also perhaps that Bach had
   consciously decided not to compete with Telemann, at Weimar or (on other

because Bach was already desiring to leave for another court? Was the senior duke concerned that chapel standards would fall, mortified to learn (if he did) that Bach was already accruing back pay at Cöthen, irritated by the junior duke's association with Cöthen (whose prince was his brother-in-law), jealous of Bach's success in Dresden (if this had already happened), and/or offended because his manner was insubordinate? None of these is implausible, nor was the quasi-feudal treatment of Bach out of the ordinary. Both dukes were dictatorial, and during the junior duke's own reign later, a horn player asking for dismissal was actually condemned to a hundred lashes and prison, and on escaping was hanged in effigy.[2] If Bach's visit to Dresden took place before his incarceration, it could have aimed at getting royal support for his request to leave Weimar, only then to offend the duke for going above his head. At least his request for release was not denied on the formal grounds that he owed money, as his admired relation Johann Christoph's had been at Eisenach many years earlier.

In 1790 E. L. Gerber, whose father was a Bach pupil during 1724–7, made what has sometimes been taken as a reference to this imprisonment when he described the *Well-Tempered Clavier* as being written – conceived? begun? – during a period in which the composer was depressed, bored and without an instrument (*Dok* III, p. 468). Or perhaps this refers to Bach's second visit to Carlsbad with Prince Leopold in 1720 (see below), when he may have had nothing much to do. Either way, Gerber Sr must have heard this from the composer himself. For the Gerbers, the point of the remark was that their hero did not need a keyboard for composing even complicated counterpoint. Portraits of Handel and Scarlatti show them seated near a harpsichord, though whether one is to understand this as their indispensable work tool or a

occasions) at Gotha or Leipzig. In 1718, six concertos by the late Prince Johann Ernst were published by Telemann: does that suggest that the latter had been much in evidence at the Weimar court in 1717, and/or had insinuated himself into the junior duke's interest, which would not have endeared him to the senior?

[2] Glöckner 1985, p. 141. The University of Leipzig had a convicted but escaped student hanged in effigy on 8 March 1723 (Schneider 1995, p. 184), shortly before the Bach family arrived in Leipzig.

mere emblem of their virtuosity is uncertain. Bach's formal portrait at Leipzig shows him holding a piece of paper containing some difficult counterpoint (a canon) – but no instrument.[3]

The Weimar junior duke's personal connection with Cöthen is almost certainly responsible for Bach's acquaintance with the prince and hence the offer of a capellmeistership. Solicited or not by Bach, the opportunity was certainly desirable: the title itself signalled promotion, Weimar was becoming problematic and the Cöthen prince was musical. The accounts do not make it as clear as is usually supposed whether Bach was paid a retainer by him from 1 August 1717, and if so whether this was tantamount to deceiving Weimar, where he had not been released and was still being paid to the end of September. Or payments could have been backdated by request and prearrangement, when he signed on 29 December (Dok I, p. 190, Dok II, p. 67). Either way, it looks from this and other circumstances as if the young Prince Leopold was anxious to have him at his court, his enthusiasm becoming part of the picture Emanuel drew later when he remarked that together with the Dukes of Weissenfels and Weimar the Cöthen prince particularly valued and rewarded his father (Dok III, p. 289).

The date the Bach family moved to Cöthen is unknown, but a guess is that it was in time for the prince's twenty-third birthday celebrations on 10 December 1717, with special music for an employer who, according to the composer, was 'as much a lover as connoisseur' of music ('so wohl liebenden als kennenden': Dok I, p. 67).[4] Though only a tenth the size of Leipzig, Cöthen offered exceptional promise, without the heavy duties of a full programme of church music.

Only two weeks after release from detention in Weimar Bach was in Leipzig to test the newly rebuilt organ of the university church, the Paulinerkirche. So much travel within a short period – Weimar–Dresden–Weimar–Cöthen–Leipzig–Cöthen – seems excessive, and

[3] Handel's portrait now in the University Library, Hamburg (1749), shows him holding a score, with a copy of Messiah on a table, but no instrument.

[4] For the juxtaposing of 'lover of music' with 'connoisseur', see below, p. 129.

one wonders whether the Dresden competition visit was not a separate trip but an excursion Bach made from Leipzig, having met up with the violinist Volumier there, and not, as the Obituary said, hearing from him by letter in Weimar. Marchand's presence in Dresden is not precisely dated. Perhaps he had left before Bach actually got there, or was already about to leave, and the colourful anecdote is a reinterpretation of events by Bach himself. (If so, it reveals a great deal.) But in any case, the effect of a hectic schedule on Bach – prison, abortive competition, relocation, organ examination – can only be guessed, for on 17 December he signed a report on the Leipzig organ that shows no sign of skimping.

In the report, he comments in good detail on the organ's overall structure, the inner working, its stoplist, voicing, tuning and key action, going on to ask that consideration be given the builder for his work extra to contract (*Dok* I, p. 165). He also recommends that a window behind the organ be covered up and a one-year guarantee signed with the organ builder. Much of this again resembles points made in Werckmeister's *Orgelprobe* and is, one might think, a little too trusting of the builder. Three important church musicians, Kuhnau of the Thomaskirche, G. F. Kauffmann of Merseburg and E. Lindner of Freiberg, had already been considered as examiners (*Dok* II, p. 69): had they declined, and if so was it because a bid of 1710 for the young master Gottfried Silbermann to rebuild totally the Pauliner organ had come to nothing?

At 2,000, Cöthen's population was tiny, the whole principality having only 10,000 inhabitants.[5] In other respects, too, it was very different from Weimar. Not orthodox Lutheran but Reformed, the court required no church cantatas and no organ music; furthermore, its young prince seems to have been something of a personal friend to the composer, which must have given the job a very different tone from previous appointments. As a teenager, Prince Leopold of Anhalt-Cöthen had toured, brought back French and Italian music, studied in Italy with a

---

[5] It is seldom clear from recorded population counts, however, whether the numbers are adults only, communicants only, householders only, etc.

competent musician, J. D. Heinichen (later capellmeister in Dresden), and played string and other instruments. Because of the last, there is a temptation to surmise that such works as the third and sixth Brandenburgs were connected at least in part with him as participant.

Although the Bach family remained regular members of the town's Lutheran church, the court was Calvinist. Becoming 'capellmeister and director of chamber music' (as the title page to the *Well-Tempered Clavier*, 1722, puts it) meant directing some sixteen first-rate musicians in chamber music and cantatas on special occasions, often with extra players. It is conjectured that some dozen cantatas were composed for birthdays, New Year, the prince's wedding in December 1721, etc. The level of musical achievement must have been higher than at Weimar, with such musicians as C. F. Abel (tenor viol player, whose son later worked in London with Bach's son) and C. B. Lienicke (cello, member of a scattered musical family), and other virtuosi on violin and woodwind. A little time before, Leopold had attracted court musicians from Berlin who had been dismissed on the succession of the philistine King Friedrich Wilhelm of Prussia.

The prince's interest in French and Italian styles might have prompted Bach to juxtapose them in his six works for violin solo, though pairing in this way was not uncommon for German composers. In addition to Telemann's constant and facile adoption of styles, Handel's first set of harpsichord suites, published in 1720, begins with a French *ordre* followed by an Italian *sonata*, neither so called but both in four movements and thus contrasted. Adopting 'national' styles must have been a natural extension of learning to work in distinct genres and to apply the details of composition specific to each. Because of these distinctions, rather than the Brandenburg Concertos having part writing and motif development that 'definitely predate the standards set by *The Well-Tempered Clavier*' (Wolff 2000, p. 232), what they are doing is realising a typical and quite different genre: the concerto grosso, to which the rigorous counterpoint of keyboard fugues is more or less irrelevant. Chronology cannot be made on the basis of such comparisons, at this or any other period in Bach's life, for his grasp of different genres and their characteristics is too firm and, in effect, compartmentalised.

What pupils Bach had in Cöthen, other than his nephew Bernard and sons Friedemann and Emanuel, is not known, nor whether he regularly played any organ in the town. Since his salary was twice and soon more than twice his predecessor's, with further payment for maintaining the harpsichord and lending his house for rehearsals, evidently he was highly valued, and chamber music must have been energetically developed under his direction. Rehearsal activity suggests at least a weekly concert, played in the throne room of the castle, but there could have been many other contexts or occasions for which incidental music was prepared and played. Unfortunately, since Cöthen's terms of employment are not known and may never have been stated, and since copies of music again belonged to the court and disappeared over time unless compiled or reused by the composer for his own purposes, one can only surmise that Bach produced many chamber and instrumental works there.

Evidently the capellmeister and five or six musicians complete with a harpsichord travelled with the sickly prince to Carlsbad, Bohemia, on 9 May 1718, where he took the spa waters and engaged in musical events, perhaps even holding semi-private concerts of a kind becoming popular in towns across Europe. It seems that the keyboard instrument taken to Carlsbad was not good enough for (solo?) concert work, because in March the next year Bach was in Berlin to pick up a new two-manual harpsichord by Michael Mietke, the Berlin court instrument maker, whose extant instruments have served in recent decades for reconstructions of 'the Bach harpsichord'.

Such an exceptional new instrument,[6] made not locally but by a builder probably recommended to the prince or to Bach by his ex-Berlin colleagues, would surely feature prominently in the prince's chamber group, along with the virtuoso capellmeister himself. Two manuals

---

[6] A Cöthen inventory of 1784 still lists the harpsichord as 'Michael Mietke in Berlin 1719' (Dok II, p. 74), i.e. this is probably what its nameboard said.

need not produce a louder sound than one, nor are they necessary for continuo work; rather, they encourage variety of effect for solo sonatas and transcriptions, trio sonatas with flute or violin or gamba, and even concertos such as the fifth Brandenburg. The big preludes of Bach's English Suites for harpsichord are so written as to make two manuals plausible, really for the first time on this scale. (Why these suites became so called is unknown. Commissioned by an English patron to whom the missing autograph was sent? In reaction to Handel's suites published in London in 1720?)[7] In 1722, Cöthen acquired another striking instrument, a harpsichord with pedals, useful for teaching, practice, concerts and composing, and even for satisfying the usual acquisitive curiosity of princes. Both instruments were surely asked for by capellmeister Bach.

It seems from the dedication of the Brandenburg Concertos on 24 March 1721 that when Bach was in Berlin in 1719 he had 'the good fortune to be heard' by the Marquis of Brandenburg, brother of Frederick the Great's grandfather.[8] Presumably he improvised harpsichord solos in a court concert of some kind, though how he came to be there – by invitation, after solicitation or through an introduction by the harpsichord maker Mietke – is not recorded. The dedication says that the Marquis, the very patron to whom twenty-three years earlier Werckmeister had dedicated his *Orgelprobe*, 'commanded Bach to send him some compositions' ('commander de Lui envoyer quelques pieces': *Dok I*, p. 216). So one may imagine a procedure similar to that of the organ sonatas compiled c1729: that is, some movements composed earlier for various occasions were collected, arranged or rewritten, and then joined by new movements or whole works to complete a variegated set of six characteristic pieces for a particular purpose.

The scoring of all six Brandenburgs, though different from one anther to an unusual (unique?) degree, may reflect current practices

---

[7] Both first suites are in A major, and both E minor suites open with a fugue; Bach's A major Allemande has distinctly Handelian details. Other German suites had also been published in London (Mattheson's of 1714): did Bach send his missing autograph to a London publisher?

[8] The dedication is in French, likely to be the work of a Cöthen colleague.

more than is often realised, collecting them in one compendium. Even No. 6's pairs of violas and gambas without violins were not unfamiliar, either in texture or timbre, in older German cantatas. No. 3 expands the notion of a string consort, now in nine parts plus bass and very different in texture from the more sombre but equally exhilerating No. 6. Together, they explicitly contrast the old (viols in No. 6) with the new (brilliant violins in No. 3), both doing so with a tremendous sense of inspired melody. Nos. 2, 4 and 5 are newly conceived concerti grossi, with a quartet and two very different trios of soloists in combinations totally new to the world of Italian concertos, their sound and Affekt again unique to each. They could well be a reaction to the more uniform scoring and sounds of Corelli's concertos Op. 6 (Amsterdam, 1712), for although Bach is not documented as knowing these works, it is hardly conceivable that Prince Johann Ernst would have brought back from Amsterdam the parts for Vivaldi's Op. 3 but not those for Corelli's Op. 6. Bach scholars seeking Vivaldi in the Brandenburgs might be looking for the wrong composer.

A further point concerns Brandenburg No. 5, for though now generally praised as the trailblazing keyboard concerto, it is neither. It is less a solo concerto than some earlier pieces by Handel, such as the sonata for solo organ, strings and oboes in Il trionfo (1707) or the harpsichord obbligato aria 'Vo' far guerra' in Rinaldo (1710). For a soloist to have so modest a role in a concerto's slow movement as he does in Brandenburg No. 5 would have seemed as odd to Handel in his concertos for organ as to Mozart in his concertos for piano. Nevertheless, there are some curious parallels between Brandenburg No. 5 and these various Handel pieces. They each have a concerto structure with solo episodes of somewhat naive, flashy broken chords.[9] These episodes can exist in more than one version, and they reflect Italian habits, even rival them. (To much the same period as Handel's Il trionfo belongs Vivaldi's concerto with organ obbligato, RV 779.) Handel in Rome was

---

[9] Note that the fifth Brandenburg's so-called cadenza is not a cadenza but the final solo episode of a ritornello movement, no doubt prompted by those in Vivaldi's Concerto for violin RV 208, already (?) arranged by Bach for organ, BWV 594.

competing with Alessandro Scarlatti, Bach in Dresden was competing with Marchand?

Having observed Handel's playing, Mattheson reported that he often turned harpsichord accompaniments in his stage works into inimitable improvised solos, during (let us hope) the episodes when the soloist was not singing (1739, p. 88). For the cosmopolitan musicians of Cöthen or Berlin/Brandenburg, to know of such Italian practices would be nothing strange. Nor would it have been strange for Bach to respond to them in his own way. He too, in playing No. 5, 'must have captivated by the lightness and elasticity of his fingers' anyone who heard him play it, as Burney said of Handel's playing in Rinaldo (1789, p. 224). Bach being Bach, however, his concerto solos could never be criticised by Burney, as Handel's were, for containing 'not one learned or solid passage'.

Unfortunately, there is no evidence that, likely though it is, the Marquis of Brandenburg used Bach's concertos, rewarded their composer or even acknowledged them, much less put him in the way of a royal appointment in Brandenburg or Berlin. This is so despite a broad hint in the dedication, when Bach describes his desire to serve on occasions 'more worthy of your Highness' ('plus dignes d'Elle': Dok I, p. 217). A Berlin student taken in by him in 1725 (Dok II, p. 218) was probably unconnected with the marquis. For Bach's later concerts in the Leipzig Collegium Musicum, the Brandenburgs' idiosyncratic and old-fashioned scoring are unlikely to have been of much use, except perhaps for Nos. 2 and 5.

In Cöthen, the period July 1719 to May 1720 saw considerable court expenditure on copying and binding music, commissioning and printing texts, and hiring musicians. These were all apparently for performances of music not otherwise documented or described. At other periods, the prince's life was marked by bouts of sickness, hence the visits to the Carlsbad spa waters (1718, 1720), and hence even the cantata texts that seem to refer to illness, which was the case at least three times during these years.

A major part of the capellmeister's job was to produce secular cantatas marking one or other event at court. It is possible that the three violin concertos best known today also originated here, inspired by fine Berlin violinists on one hand and a form of 'intellectualised Vivaldi' on the other. The concertos' movements follow Venetian models up to a point but are planned with a care and shot through with a melody that mark a development even beyond that of the Brandenburgs. The formal *types*, as for example the repeating basses in the two solo concertos' slow movements, can be traced to Vivaldi but not the density of their detail, the harmonic drive and solo violin lines. On 22 January 1720, according to its date, Bach also began the little album of keyboard music for Friedemann, then aged nine, the *Clavierbüchlein*, corresponding in format with the little album of organ chorales, the *Orgelbüchlein*, both so called as if books of instruction. The *Clavierbüchlein* would have instructed Friedemann in rudiments, notation, figured bass, fingering, ornamentation, playing and reading in many different keys, composing in certain styles and genres, and, up to a point, in extemporisation. Few glimpses of any composer's life and father's affection are clearer than the one offered here by one little piece of music: an Allemande (No. 6) which seems to have been started by the father and continued by the little boy, who could not quite get the hang of returning to the tonic without further help, which father supplied. (For further speculation on the relationship with Friedemann, see below, pp. 196–202.)

To judge by their date, organisation, character and title page, the two- and three-part Inventions were fair-copied as part of a plan of instruction, revised to be part of the curriculum for a young pupil, in Cöthen or soon in Leipzig. The title page makes the intention quite clear: through them the young musician will learn to play purely in two parts ('reine spielen': Dok I, pp. 220–1), then to manage three parts correctly and well ('richtig und wohl'); to learn meanwhile not only how to find good ideas ('inventiones') but how to develop them; and above all to achieve a singing style in playing on the keyboard ('cantable') and get a taste for composition. In a succinct way, these headings resemble Couperin's fuller programme of instruction in his book *L'art de toucher* (1716), perhaps not by chance, and the very title page suggests that Bach may have had hopes of publishing it. (For the word 'cantable', see also below, p. 163.)

4 *Clavier-Büchlein vor Wilhelm Friedemann Bach*, Allemande BWV 836.

Irving S. Gilmore Music Library, Yale University, Music Deposit 31, fols. 7v–8r. At least the title, the clefs and braces throughout, and some opening notes, are in the hand of J. S. Bach; also the last three and a half bars. The rest was probably written by W. F. Bach, perhaps (in part) recopied from a draft, hence the omitted beat in bar 4. The piece looks like an assignment: the third section is likely to be a replacement (not an alternative or supplement) to the second, which has ended in the wrong key and introduced chromatics inappropriate for such a genre. (There is a similarly inappropriate Neapolitan sixth in the third section.) Possible reasons for the last three and a half bars, surely composed by his father, are that Friedemann was at another impasse, or that such a 'mini recapitulation' after an imperfect cadence was already planned, but is now without enough space. The two final tonic perfect cadences (recalling those of the first section) make it a model close for a piece that had just modulated to the flattened leading-note minor. The following piece, another Allemande in G minor, now with its second page missing, is more in the style of earlier German allemandess (Buxtehude, Handel), rather as if it were a student's 'resit' exercise in the same key. Presumably as part of the boy's training, the G clef for the right hand in the two allemandes is unique in the *Clavierbüchlein*: a C clef is usual.

4 (cont.)

1720 also saw the fair-copy compilation of the *Sei solo* for violin, the so-called violin partitas. They are matched by the six suites for cello, probably also fair-copied and seen by their composer as a sequel, Opus 2 to Opus 1. Who played either set is not known, nor how regularly solo violin and cello works were composed by court string players at the period, whether elevated contrapuntal music of this kind or popular fiddle music. Telemann had published six sonatas for violin solo in 1715, dedicated to the young Prince Johann Ernst – that is, at Weimar. There was surely a lot of interest in such music at both the Weimar and the Cöthen courts, with solo string music that leant as much towards the street fiddler's art as towards the usual court violinist's. Both of Bach's sets look like aristocratic and newly demanding versions of the solo fiddling one would hear in the streets and taverns of Weimar or Cöthen, elevated to levels of new expressiveness by a master's control of harmony and intimate knowledge of Italian and French manners.

The orderly and systematic way Bach went about things is clear in both sets. The three violin fugues demonstrate three distinct conceptions, both of counterpoint and of form; and each partita or suite has several features the others do not (a prelude or a set of variants or a chaconne or a rondeau). The cello suites contrast six different preludes, much as the later six partitas for harpsichord do, and they also vary in instrumental requirements: No. 6 is for five strings (probably the violoncello piccolo), No. 5 for *scordatura* (top string tuned down a tone). The latter recalls the violin tuning in No. 5 of Heinrich Biber's *Harmonia artificiosa-ariosa* (Nuremberg, 1712) and earlier Biber pieces circulating via J. J. Walther, violinist at another court, Dresden. It would be odd if Biber's publication had not reached Cöthen by c1720.

The usual references to 'Bach's unaccompanied violin partitas' are doubly misleading. 'Unaccompanied', the usual English version of his title 'senza Basso accompagnato', would be better replaced by 'without a continuo part', for the violin and cello make their own accompaniment. And Bach did not call the violin suites 'partitas'. More importantly, the faultless harmony of both sets mysteriously manages to be at the same time logical, tense, moving and inherently tuneful, transporting to a unique sound-world anyone hearing just a few notes of them. A formula such as the changing chords of the Prelude of the cello suite in G major is developed into something rich and strange, as its harmonies unfold in the classic manner of a master improviser. (The unfolding harmonies of a Bach prelude for cello or violin, lute or harpsichord, organ or ensemble, are one of his best-known hallmarks: harmony so logical is automatically beautiful, and vice versa.) Whether the thoughtful calculation of these works produces music as natural to string instruments as Corelli's is a question rarely asked. But their 'system' can seem obtrusive, their art a little too artificial. It is less so in the *Orgelbüchlein*, where variety occurs more naturally since the organisation of the book follows the church year's sequence of hymns. Even there, however, one senses the composer persistently challenging himself.

Over this period work must have continued on the *Well-Tempered Clavier* Book I, yet another compilation fair-copied by the composer, who dated his grand title page 1722 (perhaps 1723 originally). Was this book further repertory for Friedemann or something prepared for publication? Either way, it supersedes J. K. F. Fischer's then well-known collection of preludes and fugues (see above, p. 71). The *Well-Tempered Clavier* also reflects common interests in central Germany at the time, to judge by a turgid oddity such as F. Suppig's *Labyrinthus* (Dresden, 1722), which is an unpublished keyboard fantasia passing through all twenty-four keys. (Marin Marais's *La gamme* of 1723 passes through only 12 keys, but does so with more musical conviction.) Some of the WTC's preludes and fugues were specially transposed for the compilation, and as with other keyboard music of these years, they could have been played by Bach to the prince on his sickbed, as, later, the Goldberg Variations were said to have been played in Dresden to an insomniac.

Some suggestions are made below (p. 176) about the WTC's musical 'programme'. Had Bach been intending a 'practical treatise on temperament', there would have been no logic in its order: a major key then its nominal minor, then the next one up chromatically, and so on up the scale semitone by semitone.[10] Similarly, the complex 'work plans' that have been conjectured for the book by modern commentators (farfetched symmetries erected on the number of bars, voices, fermatas, notes or fugal entries) do not correspond to one's musical experience of the book.

> After he had had a blissful marriage with his first wife for thirteen years, he experienced in 1719 the severest pain in finding her (on his return from a journey with his prince to Carlsbad) dead and buried, despite having left her fit and well on his departure.

Emanuel was six when his mother died and, one imagines, was not unwilling to speak in the Obituary of a 'blissful marriage' to which he owed his own existence, though the date of death is wrong (July 1720,

---

[10] The WTC preludes present in an early form in the *Clavierbüchlein* of W. F. Bach and the Inventions copied in the same album both had different orders.

not 1719). The story of his father's shock on finding her buried depends for its pathos on whether the Cöthen court payment he received on 4 July was in person or on account, for this was three days before the funeral (Dok II, pp. 68, 76). Nevertheless, whether true or not in all respects, what Emanuel describes is an experience that cannot have been unfamiliar in those days, and one that allows a little lifting of the curtain on personal feelings. Had his father spoken in these terms, and so affectingly that he misremembered his wife's death, or Emanuel his mother's?

Maria Barbara was buried with the unusual honour of the full choir of the Cöthen Latin school (Dok II, p. 76), surely on the prince's order if indeed he had returned from Carlsbad by then. As noted, it seems that her elder sister Friedelena Margaretha remained, to keep house for four children between ages eleven and five. Whether because of his wife's sad death, or because of typical quarrels between a community's clergy that dogged him in several of his appointments, or for some other reason, by the autumn of the same year Bach was looking at another job of some prestige, one with which (and with whose clergy) he was already somewhat familiar, at the Jacobikirche, Hamburg (see below).

It is unlikely that the pieces he wrote for the courts at Schleiz in August 1721 and Zerbst a year later (where he had connections by then through his second wife, Anna Magdalena) were also with a view to appointment, since they would have represented a step down. But life at Cöthen seems to have deteriorated for him when the prince married on 11 December 1721, taking as princess someone who was still being called a philistine by Bach nine years later ('eine amusa', 'a non-muse': Dok I, p. 67). Whether the situation would have improved for him when the prince became a widower in April 1723 one cannot say, for Leopold was not in the best of health himself and his finances were not flourishing. For someone with Bach's family a job in a church of repute was at least more secure, hanging less on the will or wellbeing of a prince. Though still with its dangers – clergy suspicious of organists' ineradicable contumacy – a church job offered a home and a clear contract of employment.

There is a further point here. In Bach's biography a pattern emerges in which, despite an initial enthusiasm, ardent creativity and the active support of his employer, the broad chronology of his music implies a gradual dampening of spirits in each of the jobs he held. A pattern emerges which implies that he felt less and less appreciated or encouraged for the work he originally took on with such zeal, turning then to other kinds of music about which he personally was passionate and irrepressibly productive, in this way privately satisfying his Lutheran duty to develop his God-given talent. This progression is clearest in his longest employment, Leipzig.

During this time, about 1722 [November 1720], he travelled to Hamburg and was heard there for more than two hours on the beautiful organ of St Catherine's before the magistrate and other prominent people . . . The aged organist of this church, Johann Adam Reinken . . . heard him with special delight and made him the following compliment, particularly for the chorale 'An Wasserflüssen Babylon', which our Bach, at the desire of those present, played extempore at great length (for almost half an hour) and in varied ways, just as the finest of the Hamburg organists had once been accustomed to do at Saturday vespers: 'I thought this art had died, but I see it still lives in you.' This judgment of Reinken's was all the more unexpected in that many years before he had set this chorale in the above-mentioned manner, of which our Bach had not been unaware, as he was also aware that Reinken had usually been rather jealous. Reinken urged him thereupon to pay a visit, and showed him much courtesy.

The point of this long account was evidently to show Bach as the true successor to the oldest living representative of the German Protestant tradition – again, therefore, emphasising the world of church and organ music – and it is unclear whether the Obituary authors knew that he had offered himself for a job in the Jacobikirche. Probably not, for the passage follows immediately on a remark that over this same period Prince Leopold of Cöthen had the greatest satisfaction in his work. Did Bach learn on this trip that instrumental players he could call on in Hamburg were inferior to Cöthen's, hence leaving before the full audition, saying he had to return to his prince (Dok I, p. 27)?

If Bach's interest in leaving Cöthen for Hamburg had arisen at least partly in the aftermath of Maria Barbara's sudden death, one might think Emanuel would know, especially as Mattheson had gossiped in print about the Jacobikirche organist trials of 1720 (Dok II, pp. 186–7). But perhaps he was too young at the time to know anything directly; nor is it clear how serious Bach's interest in the job could have been. The previous organist of the Jacobikirche had a salary half his at Cöthen, but fees and payments in kind were probably considerable and certainly dependable, and the church's Schnitger organ was something to inspire any organist's application. Hamburg itself, with all its city life and institutions musical and educational, must have been attractive for the father of a growing family, especially compared with the modest town of Cöthen.

Although the Obituary reported that Bach played in Reinken's church, the Catharinenkirche, the authors could have been muddled: perhaps he played an audition recital in the Jacobi, Reinken heard him there, then invited him 'to pay a visit' to the Catharinenkirche? The remark about Reinken's jealousy rings true as something told by Bach himself, but certain details in the story could easily have come from the Obituary authors' knowledge of other, printed accounts. Was it from Bach or from Mattheson 1722 (p. 256) that they knew the Catharinenkirche organ to be unusually 'beautiful'? Does the whole reference – the second one to Reinken in the Obituary – have something to do with the authors' own knowledge of his spectacularly long setting of 'An Wasserflüssen Babylon', still being copied in 1750 or so?[11] Was the remark about extemporisation made precisely because Mattheson had implied that Reinken was less of an improviser than an incomparable

---

[11] An extant copy of Reinken's chorale was made either by Bach's son-in-law Altnickol about the time the Obituary was being written or by a pupil of his (see BJ 2002, p. 42), suggesting that it was known amongst this circle.

player of pieces he had practised? This remark dates from shortly after Reinken's death in 1722, and Mattheson's account might be responsible for the story appearing in the Obituary, even for the wrong date given there.

Told at uncommon length, the story of playing to Reinken was important both to Bach himself and to the Obituary's idea of apostolic succession. Reinken's words to Bach, as quoted in the Obituary, even have something of John the Baptist about them, as readers must have realised. After all, by 1720 such chorale fantasias as 'An Wasserflüssen Babylon' were no longer familiar in Hamburg itself, and the story does rather confirm (or claim, for Leipzig readers) that traditions there had faded and that the gravitational centre had moved away from such northern Hanseatic cities. Mattheson's warm praise in his book of 1740 for the older Hamburg organists, especially Scheidemann and Weckmann, could well have prompted the Obituary authors to relate the story and so imply where the new gravitational centre was.

Normally, the phrase 'in varied ways' ('auf verschiedene Art') implies a set of variations, indeed one that could last half an hour, whereas Reinken's is a sectional fantasia of the old type, in which each section plays at length with each line of melody and shows off different parts of the organ. Most of the old 'arts of playing chorales in various ways' were being lost by the time of the Obituary, not least at the hands of its very authors C. P. E. Bach and J. F. Agricola, who knew that Leipzig had no tradition of popular organ recitals comparable to Hamburg or other cities, from Haarlem to Lübeck, in which hymn variations played a big part. What Bach would have played for a further ninety minutes – the Obituary's two unusual references to time sound like details the protagonist himself proudly recounted – is unknown but could well have resembled the scheme as laid out in *Clavierübung* III published seventeen years later, and which formed both a coherent recital plan and a programme of Lutheran devotional texts.

In one way or another the Hamburg performance was an audition, no doubt, and such trials were not uncommon in major churches. As is clear from Werckmeister's *Orgelprobe* of 1698 (p. 77), organist applicants needed to be tested in improvising a fugue on a given theme, in playing a chorale 'in various ways', in realising figured harmony and in transposing. Playing 'before the magistrate' could mean either a celebrity recital at Saturday vespers or a public trial of a short-listed candidate for an important municipal position. Equally uncertain is what playing 'at the desire of those present' means: that he played a recital not an audition, to which a ranking capellmeister would not happily submit? The phrase exonerates him from presumptuously borrowing Reinken's theme, though it is quite likely that, in Hamburg, playing this particular hymn tune 'in various ways' was expected of every candidate for every position.

The Jacobikirche organist H. Friese had died in September 1720, and the church, its Schnitger organ, its status in the city and the city's musical life (not yet obviously in decline) all offered good prospects, especially as the overall musical directorship of the city's five main churches looked to become vacant soon. It did in 1721, and Telemann was appointed: perhaps he was somehow involved either in Bach's presenting himself for the Jacobikirche job, or in his not taking it if successful. The main trial took place only after Bach returned to Cöthen. But Mattheson, who was either involved in the adjudication or made it his business to learn the details later, criticised Bach's Cantata No. 21 for its repetitive word setting ('Ich, ich, ich, ich': Dok II, p. 153), which might suggest that he had heard the cantata in a service, as a formal audition. Furthermore, over ten years later he was still quoting the famous subject and countersubject of the Fugue in G minor BWV 542 (Dok II, p. 219), as if he had heard them on that occasion. This fugue's subject resembles an old Dutch song, and for Bach to use it might – just – have been a salute to Reinken's work in the Netherlands or to 'Hanseatic interests' in general. Reinken was, after all, on the interviewing committee. Whether Bach also played the shattering Fantasia in G minor on this occasion, or indeed whether he ever coupled it with this fugue, is unknown.

The Jacobikirche committee certainly considered Bach an official applicant for the job, invited him to declare his interest in taking it, and then on 19 December learnt by letter that he had declined. Mattheson thought it was because the organist eventually appointed, J. J. Heit-mann, paid 4,000 marks for the job, thus demonstrating his ability at 'preluding better with dollars than with fingers' (Dok II, p. 187). But if Bach did refuse to pay over a sum in order to be appointed, the motive need not have been entirely creditable. For in a large Hanseatic city, where an organist could expect good social and professional status, it was not unreasonable to pay for a stake in the church's business. Prepayment could be seen as 'investing in shares' or 'buying a partner-ship' through which many extra fees for the 'stakeholders' would accrue automatically for all weddings, baptisms and funerals in a parish with a large population.

> He married for a second time, in Cöthen in 1721, Miss Anna Magdalena, youngest daughter of Mr Johann Caspar Wülken, court trumpeter to the Duke of Weissenfels. [She bore him] thirteen children, namely six sons and seven daughters.

Before moving to Weissenfels in 1718, J. C. Wilcke was a court trumpeter in Zeitz where Anna Magdalena was born on 22 September 1701. Evidently a precociously accomplished singer, she could well have come into contact with Bach before he became a widower, on some such occasion as a professional visit to one of the ducal courts in the neighbourhood, visits that both of them, as fee-paid musicians, are known to have made. Or perhaps Bach had been commissioned to find a singer for Cöthen and found her in Zeitz, at much the same period, curiously, that Handel was searching for singers. Fourteen months after Maria Barbara died, and probably earlier, Anna Magdalena was at Cöthen and a member of the Lutheran congregation. She was appointed 'court singer' by September at the latest (Dok II, p. 82), presumably on capellmeister Bach's recommendation, and evidently they were soon close enough to be married on 3 December 1721, she aged twenty, he thirty-six. However normal it was for a widower to marry at home and to buy discounted wine for the wedding, Bach did both, and reduced his expenses accordingly.

Money matters arose again a few weeks later when Bach's Erfurt connections, apparently including his elder sister Marie Salome, claimed
the legacy of their uncle Tobias Lämmerhirt's widow, which was to
have been made to Marie's brothers as well as herself. (Perhaps she
did not know they were still alive.) Sebastian objected in writing and
seems to have won his case. After his marriage he also continued to
receive a court payment each year for holding rehearsals in his house
and for maintenance of the harpsichord, which included the acquiring
of new strings (Dok II, p. 70). All this would have helped console him
for no lucrative offer from Dresden. Since the gifted Anna Magdalena –
who was something of a local diva – received a salary three-quarters
that of her new husband, and since both were more highly paid than
anyone else, the court's musical expenditure was much dominated by
husband and wife, with what ill feeling amongst their colleagues no one
knows.

Perhaps Anna Magdalena earned it well with solo cantatas in the
mould of 'Amore traditore' BWV 203. Although this one (at least, as
it has come down) is for bass, and is neither certainly authentic nor
certainly from this period, it is nevertheless a piece conforming to
Italianate chamber styles as they were known far and wide in courtly
circles – including Cöthen itself, already well before Bach was appointed. Its extravagant harpsichord part, like that of the fifth Brandenburg, doubtless typifies the kind of fanciful accompaniment Bach
and others were developing during this period. The style was illus-
trated in such books as J. D. Heinichen's *Gründliche Anweisung* (1711) and
F. E. Niedt's *Musicalische Handleitung* (1721) but is, as one would expect,
a good deal more musical and imaginative in BWV 203 than in either
of these books. A church cantata that matches the forces available in
Cöthen is No. 199, and there is a (faint) possibility that Anna Magdalena
was soloist in Cantata 194a for the prince's wedding, in the same month
as her own.

In 1722 the first of two albums of music was begun for Anna
Magdalena, comparable to Friedemann's and entitled by her 'Clavier-
Büchlein'; the second, dated 1725, continued to receive entries for

decades. The charming collection, enough of which survives to show that it was to have a mix of genres, includes some striking songs as well as (in the first book) the small-scaled and captivating French Suites. These would have furthered his wife's keyboard technique, and it is reasonable to suppose that that is what they were for. Again, both the album's songs and the keyboard suites have a character, elusive but unmistakable, that belongs only to them: a few bars of any song or any French Suite can be immediately recognised as these and not something else. (The name 'French Suites', which appears only in other copies, not here, is spurious: there is amazingly little in them resembling the Parisian norms of c1720.) While wishing to avoid presumptuous hypotheses, one can hardly help seeing the albums as tokens of Bach's warm affection for his young wife and keen support for her musical advancement. Did the first book's beginning have anything to do with Anna Magdalena's first pregnancy in summer 1722?

Instructive is the second album's versions of two partitas, very different from the sweet *galanterie* of the songs which are appropriate, in some way one can only guess, to the young woman. A 'bridal poem' written out in her hand is testimony to her happy marriage, according to Spitta (1873, p. 759), but less speculative is that, over the years, several of the youngest Bachs also worked with or in the second album. Anna Magdalena probably had new entries made from time to time for the benefit of her own children, as they were taught by their father, their siblings, herself or, most likely, by father's pupils such as B. D. Ludewig, who added a couple of pieces (BJ 2002, p. 35). Why Friedemann has no entries in the 1725 book might be explained by the now missing pages, though in any case one then wonders why they were torn out. Altogether, these are tantalising documents, and conjecture is hard to resist.

In spring 1723, just as Sebastian was involved in the Leipzig job search, Anna Magdalena gave birth to their first child, a daughter who died aged three. Seven of her first ten children died young but none of her last three. The six who survived, all of whom were born in Leipzig, were:

Gottfried Heinrich, 27 February 1724 (mentally disabled in some way)

Elisabeth Juliana Friederica, 5 April 1726 (married father's pupil J. C. Altnickol, 20 January 1749)

Johann Christoph Friedrich, 21 June 1732

Johann Christian, 7 September 1735 (the 'London Bach')

Johanna Carolina, 30 October 1737

Regina Susanna, 22 February 1742

Hints that Sebastian was a solicitous father come from documents concerning the children's training, career or abilities, areas likely to leave behind written testimony. Thus he refers to Gottfried as 'inclined to music, especially keyboard', like the older sons (Dok I, p. 261), and in a testimonial he praises a student for teaching his younger children (Dok I, p. 141). He is clearly anxious about his difficult son Bernhard (Dok I, p 107); he copies out a grand prelude and fugue for organ, BWV 541, apparently for Friedemann's first job audition in 1733; he bequeaths keyboard instruments to his youngest son (Dok II, p. 504); and he visits Berlin/Potsdam at least in part for Emanuel, whose son – the first grandson – is named after him in 1748. He also continued to work professionally with Anna Magdalena, whose singing probably continued far longer than is suggested by the scant documentation, such as at Cöthen in 1724, and whose part in teaching the children music, likewise unreported, must have been crucial.

5 Leipzig, the first decade

The city of Leipzig elected our Bach in 1723 as music director and cantor at the Thomas School. He followed where this called, although he left his gracious prince unwillingly. Providence seemed to want him away from Cöthen before the death of the prince, shortly afterwards and against all expectation, so that he was at least no longer present on this sorrowful occasion. He had the sad pleasure of preparing in Leipzig the funeral music for his deeply beloved prince and of directing its performance in Cöthen in person.

Astonishingly, these are the Obituary's only sentences about the Leipzig position, although it was the one Bach held longest and in which he produced so many mature masterpieces. The contrast with the various remarks on the Cöthen appointment, where his employer was said to be 'a connoisseur and lover of music' and where Bach performed 'to his greatest satisfaction', can hardly be missed: neither is claimed for the Leipzig position.

Nevertheless, Leipzig is an unspoken focus of the Obituary. 'Our town' is expressly mentioned in the valedictory poem appended at the end (Dok III, p. 89), and the Obituary authors, with many of its readers, knew Bach almost exclusively from Leipzig. Emanuel was only nine years old in 1723, and one can take much of what is said about Bach the

5   Cantata performance in a west-end gallery.
An engraving of the performance at the opening of Gottfried Silbermann's new
three-manual organ in Freiberg cathedral, 1714. Barely visible are choir, strings,
trumpets, timpani, lute, oboe (?), four solo singers (?) and conductor (with organ
stops behind). The nave arcade gives a narrower front to the gallery than this view
suggests, resulting in a west-end location not unlike that in St Thomas's, Leipzig, at
the time. Above, Psalm 150 gives the authority for instruments in services. Below, the
engraver is named as J. G. Krügner of Leipzig, engraver of parts of Clavierübung I and
III (see also illustration 6).

performer, the teacher and the person as concerning this period, and this period alone. It says nothing certain about him in these respects during his earlier years: the only Weimar works specified in the Obituary's worklist are the *Orgelbüchlein* and 'six toccatas for harpsichord', both probably familiar to Emanuel as he grew up.

Naturally, the Obituary says nothing about Bach being third choice for the Leipzig cantorate, although the reluctance claimed in the second sentence above is conceivably an indirect allusion to that, as when in a letter written to Georg Erdmann in 1730 the composer claimed that he had originally meant to stay at Cöthen (*Dok* I, p. 67). Since he could have dropped his Leipzig application at any point, as he had previously done at Halle and apparently at Hamburg, the claim is hard to accept *simpliciter*. So is another claim in the Erdmann letter: that it was 'not at all fitting' ('gar nicht anständig') for him to go from being a capellmeister to being a cantor.

But however fine the musical potential had once been at Cöthen, with exceptional players and an enthusiastic prince, such a position in a modest court – as a dependant, without binding contract – would not compare favourably with a regular appointment to one of the most important cantorates in Protestant Germany. Leipzig was an important city with at least three claims to great fame: unrivalled mercantile fairs, a renowned university and a massive publishing activity. Nevertheless, after six or seven years working hard in church and school in Leipzig, it is not surprising that Bach would look wistfully (as he appears to in the Erdmann letter) at a different kind of musical career elsewhere, in a town or court needing other kinds of music than sacred choral.

The Obituary's second sentence implies that being 'called' to a position was not merely a conventional, quasi-self-denigrating way to refer to a successful application but signified a dutiful acceptance of divine will. That would match other pious expressions of *Deo volente*, though one can hardly be quite sure of the matter, since claiming to have left Cöthen 'unwillingly' is just as likely to be a later gloss, the result of disgruntlement at Leipzig, even resentment at divine will. The third sentence is more clearly mistaken or misleading, since the prince did not die until 19 November 1728, nor was his ill health sudden and his death 'against all expectation'. Emanuel must have forgotten the prince's funeral music on 23–4 March 1729, in which his brother and mother took part and which included nine movements from no less a work than the *St Matthew Passion*; surely a sign that Bach had been close to the late prince.

One can certainly conclude that he came to regard the Cöthen job with greater fondness than the one at Leipzig, though how far this fondness grew from the retrospection natural to advancing years cannot be known. The Obituary's three fulsome sentences are rather out of proportion and suggest several things: that Bach spoke often of the prince and of the good connection between them, that Leipzig afforded nothing comparable, that someone so clearly successful at a prince's court was not to blame for the various vexations at Leipzig, and that the composer's intimates (including Emanuel) were only too aware of all this.

On originally moving to the job, Bach kept the Cöthen capell-meistership as a title and may well have returned to the prince on special occasions. He used this title on the first publications he ventured for himself, the harpsichord partitas Nos. 1–4, 1726–8, and prefaced a manuscript version of No. 1 with a poem saluting the prince's new-born son. A further sentence in the Obituary concerning 'the beloved prince' (*Dok* III, p. 84) again hints, in a way hardly to be missed by careful readers, that the late cantor had been better valued and happier in Cöthen than in Leipzig. Bach's not calling himself 'cantor' on official documents suggests that he kept some distance from the church when he could, liable therefore to be at loggerheads with those whose horizons were limited to it. Away from Leipzig, in a modest town such as Weissensee in 1738 (BJ 1999, pp. 22, 26), he would be known by such terms as 'the famous chapel director' or 'the famous composer Mr Bach'. It is also very likely that some factions in city, church and university governance were closer than others to the royal court in Dresden, men who wished their music director to be more of a town capellmeister (conspicuous leader of various musical enterprises) than a cantor (official of church and school).

On one hand, then, since the Obituary was published in Leipzig, perhaps it needed to say less about that part of the composer's life. On the other, his relations, pupils and admirers must have long been privy to his various grumbles, and the authors were not about either to name his antagonists or to acknowledge their support when he had had so little. But nor would the Obituary actually criticise them in print, especially when the widow needed their help. Besides, Emanuel had his own reasons for saying little about Leipzig, having been an unsuccessful applicant for the job on his father's death, as alas he was to be again in 1755.

The many-stranded order of events around the Leipzig appointment, fully documented as they would be for an important parish church, gives some idea of how a 'municipal director of music' was appointed:

5.6.1722   The previous cantor, Johann Kuhnau, dies aged 62. (As early as 1703, during a period of illness, Kuhnau learnt that Telemann had been approached to succeed him.)

14.7.1722   The twelve-member council (the *Enge Rat*) discusses J. F. Fasch (capellmeister in Bohemia), G. B. Schott (organist New Church, Leipzig), C. F. Rolle (cantor in Magdeburg), G. Lembke (cantor in Laucha), J. M. Steindorff (cantor in Zwickau) and Telemann (music director in Hamburg).

9.8.1722   Telemann auditions for the job, and is offered it two days later.

?.11.1722   Telemann declines despite an offer to compromise on teaching duties (i.e. reduce them); obtains a salary increase in Hamburg.

21.11.1722   Council considers two new candidates: A. C. Duve (cantor in Brunswick) and G. F. Kauffmann (music director in Merseburg).

29.11.1722   Schott, Duve and Kauffmann audition on Advent Sunday; Fasch declines, partly because of not wishing to teach in the school.

21.12.1722   C. Graupner (a Leipziger, court capellmeister in Darmstadt) and J. S. Bach apply.

15.1.1723   Graupner unanimously chosen, depending on successful audition the following Sunday. Rolle and Bach also invited to audition. At this point, the teaching component is omitted.

2.2.1723   Schott auditions, Rolle and Kauffmann having withdrawn.

7.2.1723   Bach auditions with Cantatas 22 and 23.

?.3.1723   Graupner fails to obtain release from Darmstadt.

9.4.1723   Council discusses Bach, Schott and (still) Kauffmann, also an unnamed musician 'from Pirna'.

13.4.1723   Prince Leopold writes graciously, releasing Bach from Cöthen.

19.4.1723   Bach (only now?) writes a letter of intent to take the job.

22.4.1723   Bach is formally elected by three authorised councils.

5.5.1723   Bach shows his Cöthen release and signs acceptance.

8.5.1723   Bach is presented to the consistory court by superintendent Deyling, who adds a testimonial (by J. Schmid, a professor of theology in the university) on the candidate's statutory theological-confessional test.

The last was no mere formality: only a few months earlier, a Zwickau organist had failed the Leipzig consistory's examination (BJ 1998, p. 27).

The council's first choice, Telemann, had withdrawn partly on the question of teaching duties in the school.[1] So did Graupner, officially for the same reasons, although at the time all three early candidates (Fasch, Telemann, Graupner) had good jobs elsewhere. Except for Handel, Telemann was probably the best-known German composer of the time, had been a student in Leipzig, and had founded the city's still functioning concert series or Collegium Musicum. For Graupner, Darmstadt had a higher prestige than Bach's Cöthen and so put him on a higher level. That Bach was in touch with one or all of the three early candidates is possible, as relations between them seem to have been good – enough for Graupner to describe Bach in writing to the Leipzig council as 'strong on the organ', 'experienced in church things

---

[1] C. P. E. Bach's candidature at St Thomas in 1755 was also rejected because of his declining to teach. But some cantors, such as Bach's brother's colleague in Ohrdruf, Elias Herda, were as much teachers of theology, Greek, Latin, etc. as musicians.

and *Capell* pieces' (i.e. cantatas for vocal and instrumental ensembles), and able to 'perform his allotted functions honestly and appropriately' (Dok II, p. 98). Whether Bach had solicited this testimonial is unknown but likely.

Some council members focused on the teaching duties attaching to the cantorate (five hours per week in the Thomasschule, plus musical instruction), some on the musical ability required, and the discussions have a depressingly modern ring to them. When by April a member speaks of having to take a 'middling' candidate because the best have withdrawn ('mittlere': Dok II, p. 92), it is not clear whether he means someone of mediocre ability or someone of only average fame – probably the latter. But eventually some councillors seem to have been swayed in Bach's favour by considering him famous enough, more so than the other candidates. As the third person in the school hierarchy, after rector and conrector, the cantor held a position of more than musical importance, so the question of a candidate's current status was not trifling.

On 19 April 1723 Bach signed a provisional undertaking to be available to take up the post within four weeks, to undertake duties in the school, both regular classes and individual singing lessons (Dok I, p. 175), and if he needed assistance for Latin classes, to engage someone at his own expense with the council's approval. He later told his friend Erdmann that he had delayed accepting the offer for a quarter of a year (Dok I, p. 67), which seems to be not quite true, unless he had taken the success of his trial performance in February, which was praised 'by all who can judge such things', as an official sign of intent (Dok II, p. 91). The normal annual income of 700 thalers he mentioned to Erdmann would not have been a huge incentive in view of the 770 he and Anna Magdalena had jointly received at Cöthen, but he was now entitled to a range of perquisites and a capacious family apartment, and even the city burgomaster's salary was only about twice as large (Szeskus 1991, p. 10). Nevertheless, as a non-graduate schoolmaster and musician his social rank in Leipzig cannot have been high and was unlikely to rise much.

At his audition, Cantatas 22 and 23 must have puzzled many of those present. For neither work, except in the finale of No. 22, has the immediate melody or easy approachability of the usual cantatas of the time, such as Handel's Chandos Anthems of 1717–18 or those soon to be published by Telemann. Cantatas 22 and 23 give the impression of a composer trying to impress with complex musical detail, such as could flatter a committee but would leave the congregation, and perhaps the choir itself, rather at a loss. These cantatas already raise two questions that lie behind the doubts some Leipzigers must have had over time about their cantor's music, leaving him in turn resentful and antagonistic. One is, was the congregation of a parish church up to recognising in Bach's cantatas and Passions – music more difficult than any they had previously known – the thoughtful meditation on Scripture that they indeed did offer to those with ears to hear? The second is a converse: if a cantata with recitative, chorus, arias, duets and chorale was too dramatic, rhetorical or affecting, and thus inappropriate in a parish church (one councillor requested that Bach's compositions be not 'theatralisch': Dok II, p. 94), was the only suitable music the kind with simple tunes, predictable harmony, standard word painting and naive rhetoric? If so, Telemann and Graupner would have supplied it much better.

On 22 May 1723 the family, complete with infant daughter, moved from Cöthen to Leipzig. This was announced in a Hamburg newspaper, as were the mode of transport (four wagons, two carriages) and the fact that the apartment for them in the Thomas School had been renovated (Dok II, p. 104). Syndicated newspaper accounts about a prime musical appointment were not rare, but since the paper reporting Bach's first Leipzig performance also gave an unusually replete report of another event decades later – his visit to Frederick the Great in 1747 – there seems to have been some special correspondent. Was it Bach himself?

Note that the newspaper also spoke of his being 'called' to the Leipzig job. If the correspondent was Bach, it is striking that he would send reports now to a Hamburg newspaper and again in 1731 (about a recital in Dresden) but not a regular autobiography to Mattheson in Hamburg, despite being asked to. His biography in the 1732 *Lexicon* compiled by his relative and colleague Walther is also brief, a fraction of the article on Kuhnau. It seems that Bach kept away from such things, but whether from modesty, immodesty, indifference, shortness of time or, in Mattheson's case, scorn is impossible to know. One can read various things into silence: had he already taken against Mattheson on an early visit to Hamburg? Was Walther compiling his book and planning its publication in Leipzig just as Bach was looking to leave? (See the letter to Erdmann of 1730, above, p. 101, and the visit to Dresden of 1731, below, p. 127.)

There seems to be a touch of pride in the newspaper's remark, supported by other documentation, that the house was renovated ('renovirte') for the family's moving in. A condition for accepting the job? Renovation reflected status, presumably, and it also implied that the cantor's rent-free housing was a benefit of great value, as indeed it was. Thanks to traditional hierarachies and the presence of school prefects, it is likely that the family was not so very affected by the choristers' dormitory and classrooms in the same building. Also, the house and its appointments can hardly have been a minor matter for Anna Magdalena, who was to have so many children there between 1723 and 1742. At that period the church house had three floors only, a successor to various buildings made at and along the old city wall, facing into a garden partly encircling the city in the place of the old moats and ramparts. Whether or not at Bach's prompting, a much bigger rebuilding was undertaken in 1731–2, resulting in an imposing five-storey block with an attic of three further storeys, cantor's apartment, study, classrooms, choristers' dormitory, and rector's house adjoining, between the school and the church.[2]

Somewhere in the house, presumably on a regular schedule, the full scores of the newly composed cantatas were used by copyists each week

---

[2] The barbarous pulling down of this building in 1903 is matched by the demolitions dating from the years of East German socialism – of the ruins of the Johanniskirche after the Second World War and of the still-standing university church in 1968.

6 Leipzig, church and school (left) of St Thomas.
An engraving by J. G. Schreiber c1735, ultimately based on J. G. Krügner's engraving of 1723 and showing the school building as it was before it was enlarged to eight floors (counting attics) in 1732. The cantor's apartment and entrance were on the extreme left of the school building, while the westernmost door into the church was presumably the cantor's, singers' and instrumentalists' entrance to the west gallery. The impression of open space is misleading: similar tall buildings occupied the viewpoint and closed in the courtyard.

to extract vocal and instrumental parts in time for Sunday (or for a Saturday rehearsal?), but the schedule can now only be conjectured.[3] Several such copyists have been identified: J. A. Kuhnau (nephew of Bach's predecessor), C. G. Meissner (who also copied various organ works), J. H. Bach (son of brother J. C. from Ohrdruf), J. L. Krebs (pupil, son of Weimar pupil J. T.) and others, as well as the two oldest Bach sons. But the part copying was only the penultimate stage. Before composing began, a set of half a dozen seasonal texts for cantatas had to be chosen, then approved by the clergy and given to a printer in time for the congregation to have the text in front of them at the relevant service. Until

[3] For example, the parts of the Whit Monday cantata No. 174 were finished the day before (see NBA I/14, KB, p. 92): when or even if it was rehearsed is unknown.

1733, payments were also made to Bach for maintaining the modest harpsichords in the large churches, St Nicholas and St Thomas (used in rehearsals rather than performances?), though whether he relegated this job to pupils after Friedemann left in 1733 is not known. Add to the ceaseless activity that all this entailed the coming and going of visitors, and one sees how apt for the family home was Emanuel's word 'dovecote'.

On 30 May 1723 Bach performed Cantata 75 'to good *applausu*' (approval? *Dok* II, p. 104) in Leipzig's largest town church, the Nikolaikirche, and on 1 June he was formally introduced to the Thomas School, where Friedemann and Emanuel were admitted two weeks later, aged twelve and nine. As Bach's letter to Erdmann pointed out, one attraction of the university town of Leipzig was that he had studious sons. Since so little is known of his previous daily life as Cöthen capellmeister, one cannot be sure how startling to Bach was his mass of duties as Leipzig cantor, though for the moment his musical emphases were certainly on the sacred. These include directing the performers for four churches, two major and two minor, and on occasion for the town council; training (and auditioning?) the Thomasschule choristers and rehearsing the choir and instrumentalists; appointing prefects for some of the music in St Thomas's (the motet without instruments) and for the two minor churches (to lead the hymns, etc.); teaching the ablest Thomasschule boys; composing and directing music for funerals and weddings (from a fund of works newly adapted each time?); overseeing the organs and their players; taking on university students as private pupils; and directing five regular and various extra events in the university church each year. Even when assistance was provided, as by prefects in copying music or monitoring the choristers, it was clearly necessary to organise a routine for such work. If prefects auditioned choristers, they still had to be supervised. Without doubt, he could have used other composers' cantatas more than he did, just as he used older music at other points in each service, and a big question is whether the compulsion to produce weekly cantatas was self-given. 'Largely' is probably the answer.

The main weekly service itself was a big event. Three or four hours long, it began at 7 a.m. with a series of musical items (hymns with prelude, motets, special works on some twenty feast days), mostly in older idioms but with the modern cantata between Gospel and Creed, perhaps with a Part II or even another cantata after the sermon. Many minor details of these services are still unclear – what exactly is a chorale prelude for? was there a big organ voluntary at the end? – but there is no doubt about the effort required. In particular, Bach's first Christmas season in Leipzig meant a massive amount of work, presumably prepared during the weeks of Advent when there was no ensemble music in services. But from Christmas Day up to 9 January some seven major services in thirteen days meant nine major choral and instrumental works, including the Magnificat at Christmas vespers. On the chief feast days the custom was for one of the main churches to have music at morning service that was then heard in the other at afternoon vespers, beginning at 1.15 p.m.: such days were Christmas, Easter, Whit, New Year, Epiphany, Purification, Annunciation, Ascension, Trinity, St John, Visitation, St Michael and Reformation. Regular congregations in the two largest churches could have amounted to some 2,000 people, and it has been estimated that the number of Bach's church performances alone over the period 1723–50 came to about 1,500 (Wolff 2000, p. 251). For so many of them, one is to imagine the literate congregation members reading the text of the cantatas as they listened to the Word in sound.

But these duties barely hindered what Bach seems to have seen as his prime duty: to compose – in the first instance cantatas, some sixty per year, the first set straightway on taking up his appointment, all of them major works. In particular the arias of the first Leipzig cantata cycle can give one the impression of a driven creative energy not always hitting a tone of natural melody and effortless shaping. If this is a fair judgment, one can imagine why: the sheer industry necessary in a short space of time. Yet these cantatas are free of 'short cuts', seldom calling on the common-property formulas of harmony, counterpoint and melody that one recognises in Handel's music when in 1717–18 he too had to write a series of cantatas to order – the Chandos Anthems. As Bach sometimes called on earlier music for the work in hand, so did Handel.

How much the differences between Handel's and Bach's work say about either composer himself is a big question. Handel could draw on Italianate idioms which, however conventional one now recognises them to be, were more or less new to English listeners, and his own inimitable touches only enhanced their immediate attraction. Bach, on the other hand, was participating in a more thoughtful musical culture in which he would make his mark by continuing the work of his predecessors at a more intricate level, outdoing them in various forms of complexity, though a complexity fortunately leavened by his immense melodic gifts. The Magnificat, from December 1723, is a work of enormous charm and complete originality, with a distinct aura to its melody, not quite like anything else, immediately recognisable. Yet just as Handel in his early English anthems adopts details of style from older London composers, Purcell and others, so Bach's Magnificat alludes subtly to the work of various earlier Leipzigers, Kuhnau, G. M. Hoffmann and J. Schelle, as well as to that of his co-applicants for the position, Telemann and Graupner.

Was Bach's first Advent in Leipzig a moment when his melodic sense began to flower? Cantata 194, a special work for an organ in-auguration in nearby Störmthal shortly before (on 2 November), gives an impression of 'much work but less inspiration' when compared with the Magnificat or St John Passion, work on which may have begun during or soon after Advent 1723.

Early in Leipzig Bach was finalising the set of French Suites for harpsichord and soon the six sonatas for violin and harpsichord, useful for the music making of his growing family. Few of the movements in these collections take 'short cuts' either, and at times the violin sonatas betray a driving earnestness and artifice, producing some ungrateful moments for the violin. However, when in 1725 Bach prepared the harpsichord partita No. 1 for publication – the first work he himself published – he was in effect showing that the 'driving earnestness' of the early Leipzig years was turning into something deft, imaginative

7 Praeludium of harpsichord partita No. 1.
The first page of music in score that J. S. Bach published: *Clavier Ubung, Partita 1, Published by the Author*, Leipzig, 1726. Previous publications, only one of which survives, were of the text and parts, in movable type, for election cantatas at Mühlhausen, 1708 and 1709, issued by the town council. Only in 1726 did Bach produce his own publication, an engraved keyboard score. Partitas 2–6 followed, and the six were republished as a complete set in 1731.

and new. Some movements in the partitas previously composed, Nos. 3 and 6, have a grinding quality (Gigue of No. 6) that is totally absent from the later and unique No. 1. This is a one-off, original masterpiece in which suite conventions have been totally subsumed in the interests of pretty, lyrical, winsome melody and harmony, both newly conceived, every movement showing new ways of writing for the harpsichord – a finer art in some ways than setting orthodox texts for a church cantata, where a fund of expressive conventions can be more readily called upon and reinterpreted.

Like suites or partitas, the cantatas (including 'chorale cantatas' of the second cycle, based on hymn texts) are most likely to consist of six or seven movements, in each case showing a simple regard for contrast as an organising principle:

cantata	suite
grand opening chorus	(a prelude of major proportions)
aria	allemande
recitative	courante
aria	sarabande
recitative	dance I
(aria)	dance II
chorale	gigue

Although there is no exact correlation between the individual genres – a final gigue seldom has much in common with a final chorale – the principle of contrasted movements, the alternation of the vigorous and the contemplative, is similar. Performers of both kinds of work still find them taxing.

General distinctions can be drawn between cantata types. Over a third of the first annual Leipzig cantata cycle are older works revised and rescored – indeed, almost the whole of the known Weimar repertory, hence our knowledge of them. For a cantata such as No. 21 four versions – only marginally different in this instance – can be identified from c1713 onwards. From Trinity 1724, chorale cantatas predominate: these are in effect sophisticated 'rewritings' of a strophic hymn so as to preserve its narrative in the form of a suite-like succession of chorus, aria, recitative and plain chorale. The treble parts are noticeably less demanding than those of the first cantata cycle, a clear sign of the practical composer: it looks as if in his first months at Leipzig he had overestimated both singers and players, including the brass players and even the brass instruments themselves. From Trinity 1725 big choruses are fewer, beyond the customary final chorale. Since this cycle also included works by Johann Ludwig Bach (eighteen, easier to prepare and perform) and a Good Friday Passion by Brauns (see above, p. 21), one might ask whether Bach was trimming his sails and reducing his commitment of time and energy, having experienced the limitations of Leipzig performers?

The Obituary's worklist includes 'five Passions' and 'five full annual cycles' of cantatas, which at first suggests that as many as 100 cantatas have been lost. Cycles three and four become increasingly sparse and five is entirely missing, unless the last part of the Christmas Oratorio is a remnant. But since the Obituary worklist includes pre-Leipzig instrumental works, its 'five cycles' might also be counting Weimar cantatas, irrespective of their revision for Leipzig. So too might 'five Passions': only four are documented – St John (1724), St Matthew (1727), a lost St Mark (1731) and a pastiche St Luke (1730) – but there is also Brauns's Passion from Weimar. By 1718, the Hamburg composers Keiser, Telemann, Handel and Mattheson had set one version of the Passion story, the libretto by B. H. Brockes, and although Bach may have tried his hand at something similar, it is now in Leipzig that he creates what is virtually a new art form. His predecessor Kuhnau had recently established a tradition for an annual Passion centred on the Gospels' own texts, in orthodox Lutheran manner, and it gave Bach his opportunity.

In view of the very uncertain documentation after the early 1730s, the question arises just how regularly cantatas went on being performed. Every Sunday till the end of Bach's life, with parts reused and/or recopied, year in, year out? Not always with revisions? Organised by the cantor or by his prefect? Did the motet with organ accompaniment increasingly replace the cantata for choir and instruments? What part did the clergy play in any change of emphasis? Details of Bach's life in this connection are strangely uncertain, over a long period of time, and the very uncertainty suggests a less rigorously kept programme as time went by. In his last years, it is possible that Passion settings, either his own or more likely works by other composers arranged by him, were performed during Lent or Holy Week, not in church vespers but in Leipzig's 'Grand Concert' series, the Grosse Concert society founded in 1743.

During the first winter in Leipzig, the St John Passion was composed for the Good Friday vespers of 1724 in the Nikolaikirche, and one can only guess what impact that uniquely touching work made. A previous Passion, Kuhnau's St Mark of 1721, is lost and cannot be compared with it, but the congregation can never have heard anything like its opening bars. Only on the most modest and local level does Bach seem to have influenced Passions elsewhere during his lifetime – for example, at Naumburg and Greiz – but neither was he much indebted to previous settings by predecessors in Leipzig or even Hamburg for St John. As with his first Leipzig cantatas, he appears to aim at affecting and moving a larger and far more socially mixed congregation than at Weimar.[4]

Three years later, the *St Matthew Passion* developed the concept even further and beyond any other work of the period, with its double choir (the result of opening out single choruses already written?) and a large *instrumentarium* that includes more or less everything but brass and timpani. A sign that the composer was concerned to realise the maximum potential effect of such works is that St John was rethought several times: the second version began and ended with choruses based on chorales, as if it were a gigantic chorale cantata; the third omitted the scenes taken from St Matthew's Gospel; the fourth (from 1749) returns to the first and most familiar form, but apparently for a greater number of performers. Bach must have made a tremendous personal investment in these two works, part musical, part devotional, works founded on the German Lutheran tradition but weighty beyond all precedent.

The *St Matthew Passion* finds the composer in a work of obviously passionate commitment, unique in its scope and grandeur, worked on, revised and later recopied in a particularly careful autograph, even with red ink for the Gospel texts and opening Agnus Dei chorale melody. That he should use ten of its movements in the funeral music for Prince Leopold in 1729 may result from more than mere convenience: he was saluting his late prince with special music, Cöthen supplied better singers, and music that was caviar to the general in Leipzig was perhaps better appreciated in a court setting. By March 1739, any resistance there might always have been (particularly amongst the clergy) to his grand Passion dramas seems to have come to a head, when the town

---

[4] Szeskus 1991, p. 53, calculates percentages in the congregation as roughly one-quarter upper/professional class, one-half middle class and one-quarter the remainder, including students.

council's clerk (why he?) informed Bach that his piece for the coming Good Friday vespers was not to be performed until he had obtained permission for it. His reported reply was that there had always been such music, that he cared nothing about it, would get nothing out of it, and that it would only mean more heavy work ('ein onus': *Dok* II, p. 339). He would inform the superintendent of the ban, though if it was the text that was objected to, they should (he implies) note that the setting had already been heard a few times.

All this suggests that someone was objecting to the text, either to the non-Gospel parts or to the way these were interspersed between the sacred text and set in rich, emotionally charged arias. If the objectors were clergy, then they were hiding behind the clerk. Either way, the composer's pique is as understandable as it is unmistakable. Both Passions were open to criticism by puritans or people of Low Church persuasion, despite the fact that no discriminating person could mistake their drama and sentiments for those of any opera. How regular their performance was after the early 1730s is uncertain, as with cantatas, but there is likely to have been a fall-off, even an indifference from the composer. Copies could be reused, it is true, but there are more documentary traces of slighter works by other composers being used than of revivals of the Bach Passion performances. Assuming that age was not accompanied by real indifference or undue indolence, the composer must still have been deeply affected by whatever reception was given these masterpieces, particularly if it had deteriorated during his years as Thomascantor.

Bach seems to have collected his non-Gospel texts for *St John* from various sources and to have relied on the Leipzig author Picander for *St Matthew* (see below), but one is hardly aware of an essential difference between them on this account. No Baroque opera begins with a sense of impending tragedy such as that of the opening chorus of *St John*, though a few cantatas move in that direction; and none leaves behind the impression of so terrible a story and such intense sadness as the final movements of *St Matthew*. It is not easy, even in Handel's operas, to find passages as theatrical as the crowd scenes in St John, but here the theatre is not a Baroque opera house but one's own imagination.

The Gospel narrative itself provides the drama, and while in principle no music is more than optional to the Passion – the Gregorian Gospel reading for Holy Saturday is a simple intonation – it is there to underline what is already written and already familiar. One particular moment in the story, Peter's denial, is instructive in this respect. Here, St John is much more extravagant than St Matthew, pulling out every rhetorical stop, wailing melismas, rising and falling chromatics, all of them conventional musical effects conveying distress. St Matthew at this moment is much simpler, brief, light, without old-fashioned rhetoric – and much more affecting.

Particularly full of *Affekt*, as if in response to the sheer sadness of the story, is the way that movements might combine the old chorale and some new poetry, as in 'Mein teurer Heiland' in St John or 'O Schmerz!' in St Matthew. Whether it was Bach himself who was responsible for this idea or the librettist Picander with whom he must have been in contact is uncertain, but it could well have been the composer. St John was performed four years before Picander published his book of cantata texts, but using complete chorales in this way was a natural extension of using bits of chorales, as in the early funeral Cantata 106 of c1707.

To respond to the trial scene in St John as Bach does, with an organised key plan, returning choruses and a sense of symmetry, is to be true to the Gospel itself, where the trial is not only central but has its own formal elements, such as the classical motif of peripeteia, or reverse of circumstances.[5] Less obviously symmetrical but as surely planned is the key scheme of St Matthew, which wanders more than once from minor to major sharp keys and through to flat keys, moving from an elegaic E minor at the beginning down to a tragic C minor at the end. The final closing discord is in theory typical of a French chaconne (as also at the

---

[5] If Jesus had only responded to Pilate in a more conciliatory way, the story could have gone in a different direction.

end of St John), but the effect here is much more painfully beautiful, long, repetitive and voluptuously scored. And yet despite the sustained and easily sensed richness of St *Matthew*, with its long prayer-like arias and its hugely colourful layout, St John has a touching quality that hits the listener from first to last, from the dreadful opening reiterations of G minor to the final, overpowering hymn. This long chorale alone is a masterpiece of uncanny music, more than a mere hymn as it moves towards its unique expression of hope.

There is a further dimension to the Passions not easily envisaged today: their story of a public execution was told for a Lutheran congregation who had witnessed public executions. New city regulations in Leipzig in 1721 (Schneider 1995, pp. 180f.) specified that a procession of heavily armed soldiers was to accompany the 'poor sinner' to the place of execution outside the gates, near the Johanniskirche; and at certain moments in the procession the choristers sang. On another occasion, wind players, presumably the same who played in the Passions, processed with workmen sent to build a new scaffold. How far Bach, like the superintendent of the Thomaskirche, was personally involved in these events is unknown, but the procedures were public, and as 'director chori musici lipsiensis' he was ultimately responsible for the music. Recent executions had been particularly grisly: a woman or 'child-murderess' on 3 December 1723 and a botched beheading on 13 February 1727 (Schneider 1995, p. 187). There were others in 1724, 1739 and 1740 (a triple execution, as in the Gospels), that of 1739 on the market place. Such events suggest very graphically that 'Ach! Golgotha' in the St *Matthew Passion* was more than an aesthetic experience of sad-sweet music.[6] Similarly, the city regulations' precise description of the military's duties underlines the important – and for Leipzigers realistic – part played by soldiers in the two Passions, ensuring judicial formality, saving Jesus from the lynch mob, scrabbling over his vestments (St John). A key moment in St *Matthew* is the captain of the guard's recognition of the 'Son of God'.

[6] The suicide of the conrector or assistant principal of the school in January 1742 must also have been a momentous event.

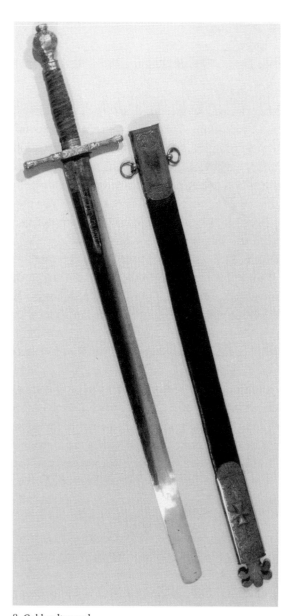

8 Gebhardt sword.
A sword in the possession of the *Sharfrichterfamilie*, or executioner's family, the
Gebhardts, from 1721, and now on display in the Stadtgeschichtliches Museum,
Altes Rathaus, Leipzig. Presumably, this was the sword used during Bach's Leipzig
period for the condemned, who were accompanied (at least part of the way) to the
place of execution by the choristers of St Thomas's.

Not long after, the Duke of Weissenfels appointed him his capellmeister.

Before the move to Leipzig, it must have been clear to Bach and his gifted wife that there were advantages in living in a city with two international fairs each year attracting a large number of visitors, and connected in various ways to the capital city of Dresden and its musicians. What it would have meant to him to be the first non-university-graduate in living memory to hold the Leipzig position is not known. Three preferred candidates, Telemann, Fasch and Graupner, had been students in Leipzig, hence their knowing enough to decline the job?

In official documents Bach continued to use his secular court titles (for Cöthen, then Weissenfels, then royal Dresden) before his assumed title 'director chori musici'. A director of music was an authority not only employed for various musical jobs but consulted in a variety of connections, also by visitors professional and amateur. Like Hamburg, where Telemann held a position of wide authority, Leipzig with Bach as director of music was a regional music centre with a range of activities from concerts to publishing, from special events to musical instruction. The appointment as titular court capellmeister at Weissenfels in 1729 could well have been the result of solicitation in the aftermath of the death of the Cöthen prince, though Bach (and presumably Anna Magdalena) had kept contacts with this important court, whose successive dukes had not been indifferent to gifted musicians. The ducal castle was the nearest major residence to Leipzig, with a splendid chapel.

It was also at Weissenfels in February 1713 that Bach had had a work performed, very soon after which the Duke of Weimar had raised his salary (Dok II, p. 36), perhaps as the consequence of his success at Weissenfels. The duties were informal and unsalaried, but how long the new title was valid is unclear: was the present of some venison from Weissenfels in 1741 (see below, p. 160) personal or official, an annual gift still being made? Did a church cantata such as No. 51, for soprano and trumpet, originate for musical tastes at Weissenfels and so aim for a particularly bright, light character? There is also a more general question about Bach's contact with the nobility: to what extent did he, in letters and acknowledgments, flatter, grovel before, woo or merely defer to dukes, princes and kings? Simple deference is the likeliest, for his flowery politeness was conventional and entirely unexceptional. Only anachronistically can it now be described as 'fawning'.[7]

The cantata BWV 249a, performed at Weissenfels for the duke's birthday on 23 February 1725, is interesting for being the first setting of a text by C. F. Henrici, the Leipzig poet known as Picander, and for being one of two rewritten forms of what was already a church cantata of mixed origins, the so-called Easter Oratorio of 1725. The other Picander work, BWV 249b, was another birthday offering, for one Count Flemming, governer of Leipzig, an acquaintance of Handel and, probably, host for the abortive Marchand–Bach 'competition' in 1717. The arias and choruses of all three works have a distinct festive feel to them, a sound more of a concert than a liturgy, suitable for the events outside church that Bach clearly relished. (He must also have known of Flemming's connection with Handel?) One hears something similar in cantatas of 1725 written in honour of two professors at the University of Leipzig, BWV 36c and 205. Both were revised for similar occasions, BWV 205 with brilliant choruses and arias, all of it dazzlingly graphic (rushing winds, etc.) and melodically inspired, like so many of the secular cantatas.

From them it is reasonable to suppose that Bach was, in some degree, an active member of certain social circles in the city. His very residence in the middle of things underlined his position, though it is difficult from incidental reports to see him as a charismatic figure quite in the way that Handel was in England. But active he certainly was, and April 1729 saw him becoming director of the Leipzig Collegium Musicum, in effect a concert series for a certain kind of public, run by a group

---

[7] As in the superficial reading exposed in one politically committed book, Edward Said's *Musical Elaborations* (New York, 1991), p. 64.

of musicians and students and, since founded in 1702 by the student Telemann, meeting regularly each week or more often during the spring and autumn fairs. The previous director G. B. Schott, organist of the Neukirche and a musician with whom Bach had good professional relations, left for Gotha in 1729. Whatever music of Bach's was played during, or even composed for, his periods as director in 1729–37 and again on and off from 1739, the Collegium must have been a big commitment for him, very willingly undertaken, no doubt, since by now the cantata repertory was rich enough for any church's demands. Any complaints about Bach in respect of his school duties at this period – that he slighted, neglected or abandoned them (see Dok II, p. 203) – could, if they were justified, reflect his priorities elsewhere. And any personal disgruntlement he felt with school or church could well have been reciprocated.

The new court title at Weissenfels in 1729, the taking on of the Leipzig Collegium and his work with distinctly new and chamber-like keyboard music – publication of the six partitas for harpsichord, completion of the six sonatas for organ – do suggest that some years after his appointment as cantor, Bach put increasing store by his activities outside church, as would any creative composer and potential job-seeker. That the Leipzig Collegium directorship went to Bach, rather than to Schott's assistant and Bach's pupil C. G. Gerlach, might have been due to the influence of burgomaster Lange, who was surely aware that many cities of the time in Europe were beginning to encourage important musical societies, where well-to-do subscribers hired a professional composer-director to run regular, mixed, up-to-date concerts. In Britain, the Music Society in Edinburgh, dating from the 1720s, was joined by others in English cities, and indeed kept better records of programmes, events and even committee meetings (*sederunt* books) than the Leipzig Collegium seems to have done.

In winter, the main Leipzig Collegium operated on Friday evenings from 8 to 10 p.m. in Zimmermann's coffee house near the city centre, and in summer on Wednesdays from 4 to 6 p.m. in the 'coffee garden' near the Johanniskirche. It was in the garden in June 1733 that a new harpsichord was to be heard (*Dok* II, p. 239). Presumably it stood in some kind of raised, covered loggia as in the pleasure gardens of London at that time, such as the Vauxhall Gardens where organ concertos were played and for which the youngest Bach son (Johann Christian) was later to write several sets of songs. No single programme of the Leipzig concerts exists, nor is there much information on their nature: was anyone paid, was the director contractually appointed as elsewhere, are we speaking of concerts as such or more informal convivial gatherings, did the harpsichord remain in Zimmermann's for other purposes, and so on? Chance references imply that local musicians, university students, visiting composers and touring instrumentalists participated, as they commonly did in musical or philharmonic societies elsewhere in Europe. The organist at St Thomas's, J. G. Görner, also held a Collegium on Thursday evenings at a similar time, in another house, according to a city guide of 1732 (*Dok* II, p. 235). The city had a lively concert life, though how freely open the events were is not clear.

Solo and ensemble suites, sonatas, concertos, secular cantatas and songs of the kind found in the Anna Magdalena Bach Books were suitable programme items, as were transcriptions. Like those elsewhere, the Leipzig programmes are likely to have been dominated by Italian chamber music, concertos and secular cantatas, and by more local imitations of the same genres, by Telemann and various Dresden composers. Known items were taken from Handel, Locatelli, Vivaldi, Conti, Porpora and Steffani (*BJ* 1981, pp. 43ff.). Few composers of Corelli's or Albinoni's generation are likely to have featured much beyond a work or two, Vivaldi and his imitators rather more. Bach's own contributions, presumably sonatas, concertos, arias and songs composed or rearranged for such concerts, were all Italianate to a greater or lesser extent, though not particularly up to date.

Although Italian music was the staple fare, the solo harpsichord concertos BWV 1052–1057, written out as a set by the composer c1738, are easy to imagine being performed in the Collegium concerts by one or other son or pupil – perhaps in 1739 when Friedemann paid a month-long visit to Leipzig with two lutenists from Dresden, including the renowned Sylvius Weiss (Dok II, p. 366). Or by Friedemann and Emanuel in their burgeoning careers elsewhere? The composer continued to work on the score, making changes in certain figuration as if he was working out for himself how to give the comparatively soft-voiced harpsichord (or fortepiano?) a solo role in ensemble – how to make a true keyboard concerto, in fact. The copy would have had to be recopied for an engraver if publication was intended. It is a curious coincidence that 1738 was also the year of Handel's Op. 4 concertos, published as a set 'for organ or harpsichord' and strings, and like Bach's compiled from a variety of sources, one of them for quite another instrument (harp). Although there is no evidence that Bach or the Collegium musicians knew these Handel works, they caught the public taste for new kinds of solo concerto, had a huge sale and have never been out of print.

In no real sense was either composer anticipating the classical piano concerto with these works, but rather conveying by busy figuration how the keyboard might, like the violin, participate in a consort and step forward from time to time with its own solos. Here again is a Bach genre with distinct kinds of melody and, time and again, a rhythmic liveliness through which it is almost impossible for a listener to sit still. In the case of the exquisite double, triple and quadruple harpsichord concertos, the sound-world they create is again very much their own, elusive, unlike anything else, even string concertos by himself or Vivaldi. Though perhaps specially transcribed from string concertos for his two eldest sons before they left home in 1733–4, these various concertos have – to be subjective for a moment – no rivals before Mozart's piano concertos of 1784–6.

How suitable for the Collegium were the earlier six sonatas for violin and harpsichord is uncertain, for though called 'sonatas', and therefore, as usual when Bach used this word, Italian in conception, the virtuosity they require is not for the sake of flashy Italian rhetoric but for a counterpoint as carefully wrought as that of the six sonatas for organ, which at times they resemble. If they were Collegium music, it was the *Kenner*, or connoisseurs, in the audience who would most have liked them.

6 Leipzig, the second decade

In 1736 he was named Royal Polish and Electoral Saxon Court Composer, after he had previously let himself be heard several times publicly on the organ in Dresden, to great applause, before the court and music experts there.

'Court composer' was an honorary title, probably in recognition of significant works offered to the king by the music director of his kingdom's second city: it did not denote a functionary such as capellmeister, concertmeister, *director chori musici* or even court organist. A Dresden newspaper of 1 December 1736 reported the visit and made the same three points: the organ playing in public, the 'special admiration' of the crowd of listeners, and the court appointment. Once again one is left to wonder if the Obituary authors knew such details – otherwise rare for them – from a preserved newspaper cutting, and neglected other public successes of Bach because they had no evidence of them in print. No wonder that the highly selective nature of the Obituary, which presumed on its Leipzig readers knowing something of their late cantor's life, led Forkel, the first full biographer, to ask Emanuel so many more personal questions!

In a note of 27 July 1733, three weeks or so after the court mourning for the late Elector of Saxony had ended, Bach sought a title from his successor, Friedrich August II, doing so in a petition attached to a set of

parts for a Kyrie and Gloria, parts copied by himself, Anna Magdalena, Friedemann and Emanuel Bach. These were the opening movements of the so-called Mass in B minor, probably composed over that period of mourning in readiness to present to the new monarch. It is also possible that a visit to Dresden in September 1731, or even a recorded absence from Leipzig in March 1729, had been in connection with the capellmeister's position at Dresden. The incumbent, J. D. Heinichen, died in July 1729 after a sickness, and only two years later did the young J. A. Hasse (unofficially) take up his position. Bach then went to Dresden to hear the premiere of Hasse's opera *Cleofide* and to play some recitals, both at court and in the church next to the elector's residence, the Sophienkirche.

In this same church, where in summer 1733 Friedemann had become organist, the Kyrie and Gloria may have been performed. And back in Leipzig over the following months, Bach also wrote and performed several major cantatas in honour of the royal family (BWV Anh. I 12, 213, 214, 205a, 215). In particular, Cantata 215 was given a grand evening performance in the open air, with a procession, torches, students, marshals and so forth, and found great favour with the king, who, to the evident surprise of the town chronicler (*Dok* II, p. 250), actually stayed to listen to the music. In the Leipzig Collegium concerts, too, Bach is likely to have consciously developed connections with Dresden musicians, more than likely engaging in the 'game of

←—————————————————————————————————

9 Dresden, view downstream from right bank, by Bernardo Bellotto ('Canaletto'), c1750.
The dome on the left is of the Frauenkirche; to its right are parts of the royal palace, containing the chapel associated with Heinrich Schütz's polychoral works. Further to the right is the large Hofkirche or Catholic Court Chapel (1739–54), in which Silbermann built his last major organ, and for whose dedication the completed B minor Mass might have been intended. Friedemann's church of St Sophia is out of sight behind the palace, while the opera house of 1719 is just behind and to the right of the Hofkirche. On the right bank lies Dresden New Town (Dresden-Neustadt), where Zacharias Hildebrandt, builder of the organs in Störmthal and Naumburg known to Bach, signed a contract in 1754.

reciprocated invitations' still known to many an organist today: they come to Leipzig, he goes to Dresden.

All this on Bach's part suggests an active soliciting for title or function, although nothing came through until 19 November 1736. Was this because his title as capellmeister in Weissenfels lapsed only in June 1736, on the death of Duke Christian? In that case, any earlier approach to the king would have been for a job rather than an honorary title? Meanwhile, the 'royal' Leipzig cantata music was not wasted: much was reused for arias and choruses in the Christmas Oratorio, performed in the period from Christmas Day to Epiphany 1734–5. There was nothing unusual or improper in this. Festive music was festive music, and in the days when a monarch was God's annointed, what was suitable for a new-crowned king in Dresden was suitable for the newborn king in Bethlehem. (Though not vice versa: Bach's parodies almost always go in one direction only.) The very motifs of text and music were versatile: an echo aria with pastoral overtones serves Hercules in his search for virtue in one cantata as well as it does the Christian soul in its search for salvation in another. And yet, although the melodious style of these congratulatory cantatas was mostly just as appropriate for Christmas, not all of it was: the gavotte chorus originally closing BWV 213 and apparently intended to open Part V of the Christmas Oratorio was then discarded and replaced by another chorus, just as catchy but less obviously an original dance finale.

The Obituary authors probably took it for granted that when Bach travelled to play fine instruments and/or test an organ and/or play an inaugural recital, he would take one or more of his bigger organ works with him, impressive preludes and fugues written or (generally?) revised and specially paired for the occasion. The likely gestation period of Clavierübung III (published in 1739) is close enough to the Dresden visit of 1736 for one to think that indeed it represents an 'ideal organ recital programme' of the kind Bach played, perhaps even at this very Dresden recital. Its plan is as follows:

a majestic prelude of large proportions, concerto-like in shape
a set of extensive chorales interspersed with smaller settings
some intricate, 'textbook' counterpoint (the Four Duets)
a monumental three-section fugue.

The whole comprises twenty-seven works (like Luther's New
Testament) and is based on a corpus of theological doctrine (Luther's
mass and catechism hymns), something rather different from the
model hymnbook on which the *Orgelbüchlein* had been based. Alone
amongst the *Clavierübung* volumes, Part III was 'prepared for the lovers
and particularly connoisseurs' of such music, while the others were
only for 'the soul's delight of music lovers'. Whether or not Part III
is an actual programme, complex and unworldly like the first Leipzig
cantatas, the report of 'great applause' at the 1736 Dresden recital fits
in with other testimony of the time, as Bach earns the reputation of an
incomparable organist and contrapuntist. Alas, there is no comparable
report of how the Mass movements might have been received, though
these first two movements alone scan an encyclopedic range of styles
in a mature, confident idiom that is indeed more approachable than
that of *Clavierübung* III.

Bach had also been examining or inaugurating other organs since
becoming cantor in Leipzig. There is no record of solo organ music
being played when the village organ (still extant) in nearby Störmthal
was inaugurated in November 1723 and Cantata 194 was performed, but
doubtless it was. This is also the case with visits to Gera Salvatorkirche
in June 1725, Dresden Sophienkirche in September 1725 and 1731
(Silbermann organ), probably Weissenfels in 1725 and 1729, Kassel
Martinikirche in September 1732, Mühlhausen Marienkirche in 1735
(where Bach's son J. G. B. Bach had recently been appointed), Altenburg
in 1739, Naumburg in September 1746 and Potsdam in 1747. Although
at the last three of these there was a new and celebrated instrument,
lesser organs were also involved, including some in Leipzig itself and
environs (Johanniskirche 1743, Stöntzsch 1731–2, Zschortau 1746). It
seems that autumn was a popular time for such visits. By chance, a

10 Organ keyboards.
The console layout of a major two-manual organ of Saxony in the 1730s (St Peter's,
Freiberg, organ by Gottfried Silbermann, c1733). The manuals' four-octave compass,
C–c''', and the manner in which they are recessed in the front of the organ were still
largely standard, as were the type and position of the stop-knobs, though their
number here is larger than usual. Below was the straight pedalboard of two octaves,
C–c'. Music needing more notes must have been altered in some way, or rejected.

copy of the masterly Toccata and Fugue BWV 538 mentions the Kassel
visit, giving a hint that on such occasions as a public inauguration,
a distinguished organist would prepare a distinguished solo piece or
two. The toccata seems to have been one of the pieces played before
the young Prince of Hessen-Kassel, inspiring an eye-witness account
published over ten years later (Dok II, p. 410).

For Naumburg, where today the recently restored organ gives the
best impression of a major instrument surviving from his later years,
Bach seems to have recommended the builder Hildebrandt (Dok I,
p. 113), a former pupil of Silbermann. Since the tonal quality of surviving instruments by Hildebrandt and Wagner does not, in my view,
quite compare with that of Silbermann, an interesting question is
whether Bach preferred the former to the latter and if so why. Because
Hildebrandt was more amenable on such matters as tuning and the

stoplist, or had fewer contractual commitments than Silbermann, or (like Bach) preferred heavy bass tone, or at Naumburg was content to build in an old double organ case, as Silbermann would not have been? Any of these reasons is possible.

One can suppose that in Dresden in December 1736 it was not only the new Silbermann organ in the Frauenkirche that Bach played but also harpsichords in the apartments of such courtiers as Count von Keyserlingk, an acquaintance later associated with the Goldberg Variations and, perhaps, one who had approached the king at Dresden on the composer's behalf. A plausible guess is that Bach brought his latest publication with him on that visit too, Part II of the *Clavierübung*, playing the Italian Concerto and the B minor Ouverture from it, in public or private, both works giving a marvellous expression of up-to-date Dresden tastes – for 'Italian vigour' on one hand and 'French suavity' on the other. Not only had the style differences between French and Italian music been of interest to him for thirty years, but these two works reflect the growing interest in two-manual harpsichords in Germany, particularly in Dresden, home of the Gräbner family of harpsichord makers. There are moments in the B minor Ouverture that suggest Bach was (at last) wishing to imitate a crucial element of French harpsichord style: the emphasis on the tenor part of the compass, creating the rich tessitura in which French harpsichords had long shone.

It must have been in the period following the royal appointment that work went ahead on *Clavierübung* III and on parts of the *Well-Tempered Clavier* Book II. Both suggest how alert Bach was to music of great worth, old or new, his own or that of other composers. *Clavierübung* III is an organist's equivalent to the Kyrie and Gloria of the B minor Mass, and in its plan, use of plainsong and contrapuntal ingenuities salutes the immensely subtle music of an old classic he had known for a quarter of a century or more, Frescobaldi's *Fiori musicali*. The *Well-Tempered Clavier* Book II (as it is called, though not certainly by the composer) gradually includes pieces in the various *galant* idioms *à la Dresde* that had made a strong impression on him. Thus the F minor prelude has sighing motifs, a modern key, a modern time signature (2/4), binary form, simple phraseology and distinct melodic charm. The idiom of the B major prelude is striking in another way: it is ideal for the new forte-piano, with just the right textures, variety and snatches of singing melody. Yet in neither work is Bach satisfied with the unadventurous harmony, simple repetition and general tendency towards easy solutions typical of so much up-to-date music c1740.

Some of his contributions to the Schemelli Hymnbook of 1736 also have a modern, even *galant* flavour, delightful, straightforward and thus as different as can be from the published keyboard music, with its unheard-of complexity both as composition and as music to play. Also shot through with modern touches is one particular cantata of the time, No. 30a, composed in homage to a local lord, a *dramma per musica* (according to the printed text) with *personae dramatis*, catchy tunes in 2/4, a startlingly suave flute aria and dance arias. The step from this to opera is not huge, giving admirers now, and perhaps the composer himself, many deep regrets that this was never to be.

In the case even of the Goldberg Variations (published 1741), there is one detail amongst its many complexities that is as thoroughly modern as anything in the latest opera or mindless Italian violin sonata: its simple phrase structure. Not the least startling thing about the Goldbergs is that the Aria and all thirty variations (with a few excep-tional moments in certain canons) are made up of two-bar phrases, over and over again, cleverly integrated, each section being moulded into a coherent whole. Considering that the thirty-two movements are con-structed in two exact halves of sixteen bars each, the two-bar phraseo-logy seems to be courting disaster, a symmetry too far. But the solving of this self-given problem, typical of J. S. Bach, seems effortless, and one is barely aware that it is there at all.

After Bach's successive Dresden visits, it is possible to sense changes in his musical language. Soon after the visit in September 1731, an older cantata, No. 70, was revived, hard to distinguish from other early Leipzig cantatas and thus bringing with it the earnestness typical of the first cantata cycle. But the following week a newly composed cantata was sung, BWV 140, as carefully wrought as earlier cantatas but now much more immediate and easy to grasp, and containing one of the composer's best-known tunes (the chorale movement 'Wachet auf'). In its two duet arias this cantata develops the traditional dialogue of Christ and the Soul much farther than usual, indeed in the barely veiled erotic language of opera. Like the Song of Solomon to which much of the text alludes, it seems to be challenging the believer to hear the spiritual in the amatory. One can imagine Bach, both as a man and as a composer, being interested in a particular musical challenge: amatory dialogue as spiritual dialogue, the lower purposes of existence subsumed in the higher.

Reminiscent of arias in Hasse's Dresden operas, especially those in 2/4 time, are several in the secular cantatas BWV 213 and 214, performed a few months after the 1733 Dresden visit and, as already noted, reused for the Christmas Oratorio a year later. The immediately different sound-world of this oratorio when heard after either of the Passions is not simply a matter of chronology and subject matter but of Dresden tastes, now newly and richly transformed.

Perhaps it was from working with a spate of gifted pupils around 1740 – such as Goldberg and C. F. Abel (who came to London), or the writers Kirnberger, Agricola and Kittel – that Bach seems to have developed two quite different modes of music in his later years: the *stile antico* or quasi-Palestrinian counterpoint as formulated in Fux's *Gradus ad Parnassum*, and the *style galant* of simple melody and harmony as found in the work of Pergolesi or various Dresdeners. The very contrast between these two modes, roughly demarcating sacred and secular repertories, was characteristic of Dresden's musical life, which was broader and livelier than that of Leipzig. Its court composers are likely to have been visited by foreign musicians even more often than J. S. Bach was visited by them in Leipzig. A visitor to Leipzig in 1749, James Hutton, might bring back a copy of the Goldberg movements (those used by Hawkins in his *History of Music*, 1776), but later visiting musicians from England, such as Charles Burney in the 1770s or Edward Holmes in the 1820s, found Dresden of far wider significance.

The interest shown by Bach in so many kinds of music – an interest still not fully documented – lasted his whole life and took various practical forms: owning collections (e.g. a manuscript of Palestrina masses from the Weimar years), copying foreign music and its notation (Grigny), reworking whole movements (Corelli) or their themes (Raison, Legrenzi), transcribing whole works (Vivaldi), 'completing' others for performance (bass and instruments for Palestrina's mass *Ecce sacerdos magnus*, c1745) or arranging them (Pergolesi's *Stabat mater*), even into his final years (a further cantata by J. C. Bach †1703 or J. L. Bach). Since he also acted as agent for other publications than his own, is one to suppose a little stock of such items as the following, for sale in the Leipzig cantor's office?

Clavierübung I–IV
eventually the Schübler Chorales, *Musical Offering* and Canonic Variations
Hurlebusch, *Compositioni*, 1735
Heinichen, *General-Bass*, 1728
Walther, *Lexicon*, 1732
J. L. Krebs, *Clavier-Ubung* III, 1741
W. F. Bach, *Sonate*, 1748

In 1738 he also made his one known subscription to a publication of music, Telemann's Paris Quartets. All such activity with other composers' music again puts in a somewhat different light Handel's purloining from composers abroad, some of whose themes he used (and generally improved) as if from memory. Today's well-researched composers such as Bach and Handel have necessarily left many pieces of evidence for borrowing in some form or another, but they were surely not exceptional.

That Bach was not an agent in the 1730s for G. F. Kauffmann's important collection of organ chorales *Harmonische Seelenlust*, at least not according to its title page, is striking. Engraved by J. G. Krügner who also worked for Bach, published and sold in Leipzig in ten issues over the very years *Clavierübung* II and III were appearing, this big collection's ninety-eight settings are amongst the most competent organ music by any contemporary. Kauffmann had been a rival candidate for the cantorate and was a colleague of Friedemann's violin teacher Graun, so their acquaintance is not in doubt. His collection gave far more information than Bach's bare volumes did, laying out the chorales as actually performed, and adding both organ registrations and a useful introduction. To publish organ music in Leipzig without involving Bach seems to imply something, but what? Did Kauffmann not ask? Did Bach decline? If so, it cannot have been on grounds of quality, for Hurlebusch's efforts are feebler. Perhaps their previous rivalry had resulted in estrangement; or Kauffmann's famous, large instrument in Merseburg (which inspired his registrations) occasioned envy; or his first issue in 1733 persuaded Bach to go his own way instead and think about publishing chorales of his own for the first time.

Bach's 'retail agency' may have been more active than is now known. For while one cannot imagine Handel ever selling a piano, a receipt of 1749 suggests that Bach did exactly that – his own or, more likely, one for which he acted as agent, dispatching it to a buyer in White Russia (*Dok* III, p. 633). The receipt may represent the tip of an iceberg, being also a further piece of evidence for the composer's contact with aristocrats from Slav countries.[1] Another activity sparsely documented but probably quite an active business was the hiring-out of cantata parts, not least to organist relations elsewhere. As is clear from a letter to his cousin Elias in 1748, Bach would also expect payment of postage when letting a relation have a copy of a work (see below, p. 146). His business activities and, in particular, the very possibility that he was an agent for the sale of pianos, jar against many a Romantic picture of the composer.

One problem with music in the more modern idioms of the 1730s is similar to that with Bach's earliest works: both are hard to distinguish from work of contemporaries. *Galant* chamber works such as the Sonata in E flat major for flute (reliable sources) or the Sonata in G minor for

---

[1] In this instance, Count Jan Klemens von Branitzky in Białystok. Others were Hermann Carl von Keyserlingk, Russian ambassador in Dresden; Franz Anton von Sporck in Lissa, Bohemia; and Adam von Questenberg in Jaromerice, Moravia.

violin/flute (less reliable) could be either genuine Bach works written in the style of younger composers, or music of a younger composer familiar with genuine Bach works. The flute sonata in E flat could be the work of Bach imitating Quantz or that of a younger composer familiar with Bach's organ sonata in E flat. Writers now can and do find reasons for preferring one of these possibilities to the other, and only newly discovered source details would settle the question. What is certain, however, is that when an indubitably authentic work does adopt the *galant* style, as in the slow movements of the Sonata of the *Musical Offering* (1747) and the Triple Concerto in D minor, there still lurks Bach's relentless tendency towards contrapuntally conceived harmony, unshakable and inimitable. These works are up to date but could not possibly belong to anyone else.

7 Leipzig, the final years, and the first personal descriptions

In 1747 he travelled to Berlin and on this occasion had the opportunity of having himself heard at Potsdam before His Majesty, the King of Prussia. His Majesty himself played over for him a subject for a fugue, which he at once performed on the piano [auf dem Pianoforte], to the particular delight of the sovereign. Later on, His Majesty desired to hear a fugue in six real parts, which command Bach also fulfilled immediately, on a theme chosen by himself, to the wonder of the king and the musicians present. On his return to Leipzig, he set it down on paper and dedicated it, engraved on copper [the Musical Offering], to the king.

The 1730s had seen further work in composing, arranging, copying out and performing chamber music, including the harpsichord concertos BWV 1052–1057 and 1058, much of the output no doubt for Collegium concerts, of which Bach took up the directorship again from October 1739 for a further period. A chamber-like style is clearly in his mind at this period: even the big Credo chorale in Clavierübung III betrays an interest in modern sonatas, as the Well-Tempered Clavier often does in the new galant tastes. Church work continued, not without moments of chagrin, and the last decade saw a series of other composers' sacred works adapted and performed in Leipzig, including Handel's Brockes

Passion. These arrangements are known from copies or chance reference. Perhaps many more were introduced, and if so, a greater range
of music was heard in St Thomas's than in, say, St Paul's, London, or
St Mark's, Venice. How far this turning towards other composers reflects on Bach's part exhaustion, indifference, a failing drive or a more
positive wish to enlarge repertory is not at all certain, and could be
understood in many ways.

Professional visits of various kinds also continued, including one
to Weissenfels with Anna Magdalena in 1739, one to Berlin in August
1741, where Emanuel was court harpsichordist to the king, and one to
Dresden in November 1741, where Friedemann was organist and Count
von Keyserlingk his host. Such trips must have meant considerable
foreplanning, arranging for deputies, lengthy and expensive travelling,
and always the risk of ill health for himself or one of the family left at
home. While away in August 1741 Bach was told by letter of Anna
Magdalena being seriously unwell, surely giving him presentiments
after the experience with Maria Barbara in 1720?

One reason for such trips was to develop contact with potential patrons, as in Berlin in 1741, when the wedding cantata BWV 210 may have
been sung. Another was support for his professional sons: to Dresden
in 1733 for Friedemann, or Mühlhausen in 1735 and Sangerhausen in
1737 for Johann Gottfried Bernhard. Letters to Sangerhausen in 1736
concerning Bernhard's application there not only draw on past contacts
but twice ask about the salary, suggesting that money matters arose
for perfectly sensible, professional reasons. Similarly, when Bernhard,
then aged twenty-three, reneges on debts, his father will not pay unless
he sees a signature of liability, and he wants to know whether Bernhard
left any belongings behind when he fled (*Dok* I, pp. 108–9). There is
both solicitude for this son and a willingness (if circumspect) to accept responsibility for him, and he appears distressed when Bernhard
moves on without letting him know where.

Support for Friedemann might have been behind the trips to Dresden
in 1736, 1738 and 1741, in connection with the spectacular new
Frauenkirche and its Silbermann organ, two outstanding masterpieces

of Baroque art and artifice. In 1736 the Frauenkirche was new, but local musicians held the organist's position until February 1742, when Friedemann could well have expected to be promoted to it. Was his father absent from Leipzig in February 1742 because of a further Dresden visit (Dok II, p. 400)?[1] As one would expect, the Obituary gives no hint of any favouritism for Friedemann, though it was probably being compiled while he was in Potsdam, delivering their young brother Christian into Emanuel's family – and perhaps handing over a file of press cuttings.

If the Goldberg Variations appeared in print just before the Dresden visit of 1741, as is now supposed, doubtless Bach took along copies for Friedemann and Count von Keyserlingk, and a question is whether they were actually composed for the count (so that his young harpsichordist J. G. Goldberg could play to him during sleepless nights, as reported in Forkel 1802) or for Friedemann himself, a brilliant player in a brilliant city, and at some point young Goldberg's teacher. Although Friedemann was probably Forkel's source of information, there is no record of a commission, and during the work's gestation Goldberg would have been only twelve or thirteen years old. A dedication to Keyserlingk could have been added on a special copy, it is true, but as likely is that Friedemann's abilities occasioned the work, and that he liked weaving an anecdote around it later, especially if Goldberg did subsequently make such use of it.

The visit to Potsdam on 7–8 May 1747, which perhaps Keyserlingk again facilitated, is the last public appearance recorded by the Obituary and is full of implications, about both the event and its reporting. The Berlin notice of 11 May, republished in other regional newspapers, is the one and only time Bach featured on the front page of a newspaper (see Dok II, opposite p. 401), but the visits to Frederick of men renowned in the arts and philosophy were generally given good publicity, since Berlin

[1] Early in 1742, the Silbermann organ in the Frauenkirche had developed a structural fault. Perhaps either or both Bachs were consulted.

newspapers were copied around Protestant Germany. (Four years later Voltaire famously came to take up residence, though inevitably quarrelled with the king.) No account makes it clear where exactly in Potsdam the meetings took place, for more important to the newspapers was the picture of Frederick, ravager of Silesia and Bohemia, being so artistic that he himself composed the theme for an event he was still recounting to the Austrian ambassador nearly thirty years later (*Dok* III, p. 276). The Obituary supports its own hero by claiming the second recital's theme to be Bach's, but this, like its account of the incomplete *Art of Fugue*, may be a misunderstanding – the authors were drawing on the ambiguous account in the newspaper (*Dok* II, p. 435), although Emanuel had presumably been present and knew the *Musical Offering*.

Together, the newspaper and Obituary relay a crucial detail not found in Bach's own dedication to the *Musical Offering* – that it was on the pianoforte that the king played over his theme. Bach spoke only of 'Clavier' (*Dok* I, p. 241), but for the newspaper so up-to-date an instrument as the pianoforte was a valuable sign of Frederick's modernity. It was later said, apparently by Friedemann who claimed to have been with his father on this occasion, that in effect Bach had been invited by the king (Forkel 1802, p. 9), but neither Obituary nor newspaper says so. Either way, some idea of the composer's energy and sense of an honour conferred is given by fact that the *Offering* was conceived, composed, assembled piecemeal, engraved, presented and on sale by the time of the Michaelmas Fair 1747, only four and a half months later.

The whole occasion, though royal and therefore grander than most, must speak for many such musical events. A famous capellmeister – this is the newspaper's phrase, 'cantor' being inappropriate here – visits a court, is invited to play at one of the regular evening chamber concerts, sits down at the keyboard and improvises at length, to the conventional astonishment of those present. Then on his return home, in further obeisance to royalty, in the hope perhaps of preferment (a title? pension? sinecure?), and surely in response to such an interesting theme, the composer works further on it, saluting his patron's connoisseurship by including pieces both uniquely complex and stylistically fashionable.

Their appearance in print – something by now much less exceptional than it would have beeen at the time of the Brandenburg Concertos – would not absolve the donor from presenting a special, unique copy to the royal patron. Such a series of events must have occurred countless times across pre-revolutionary Europe, and here the newspaper was establishing two things: how enlightened a liege-lord its readers had, and how uncommonly gifted was this particular German composer.

Whether Bach was by now so very renowned is less clear, for the report in the newspapers was exceptionally detailed (see BJ 2001, pp. 95–6), making one wonder whether Bach himself instigated it. Or was Gottfried Silbermann, maker of Frederick's fortepianos, the correspondent? If Silbermann was the first to use the term 'Forte und Piano' in Germany, as seems to be the case, the report from Potsdam was a fine advertisement for him. And if it is true, as J. F. Agricola reported decades after his student days in Leipzig in 1738–41, that Bach had found the treble tone of Silbermann's earlier instruments too weak but gave them his complete approval after they had been improved (*Dok* III, p. 194), perhaps he publicly expressed this new view at Potsdam in May 1747. And if the king played over his theme on the piano and Bach took it up at the same pitch, then one understands why the Ricercar à 3 begins in the upper soprano range of g′–c‴, which is uniquely high for a three-part fugue by Bach.[2] This very part of the fortepiano compass would be what Silbermann had by now mastered, giving it that sweet, pearly tone one hears also in Viennese pianos of Mozart's time, and used by him for seductive melodies in his piano concertos.

Especially in view of the softness of early pianos – always more *piano* than *forte* – the treble part of the compass was problematic, impossible to make sound well without stronger strings and structure. Nevertheless, contrasts either sudden (*forte/piano*) or gradual (*crescendo/diminuendo*) were possible within certain margins, and there are many places in the Ricercar à 3, as in the more *galant* preludes

---

[2] Compare this with the Chromatic Fugue in D minor or with fugues in the *Well-Tempered Clavier*. Is the high-lying G major fugue in *WTC* II also, therefore, a piano piece?

and fugues in WTC II, where dynamic change is feasible. Also, just as the canons of the *Musical Offering* would flatter Frederick's scientific musicianship, and its four-movement Sonata his up-to-date Italianate tastes, so using the flute in a difficult key – C minor – was both a challenge and a recognition of the king's ability as a player. Especially as Frederick's flautist and teacher Quantz had worked with him on various improvements to the flute's construction, it seems the *Musical Offering* was as much prompted by recent instrumental technology as by Potsdam's exceptional group of gifted performers.

The king's theme does suit both the disciplined counterpoint of the Ricercar à 6 and the flashier, looser treatment of the Ricercar à 3, at least for a composer able to explore both. Their complementary nature is characteristic of J. S. Bach's way of pairing different styles, and the only doubt is whether Frederick himself composed – surely not improvised – this outstanding theme. Mindful of his image as artist-philosopher as well as soldier, and in expectation of the visit, he could well have been prepared beforehand by one of his musicians, his teacher Quantz, for example. The theme contains several common-property formulas found in fugue subjects of the time and yet cannot itself be treated in canon, which one would expect of an original Bach theme, given his many canons of that period.[3] Either way, the theme's chromatics give the work another of those unique auras characteristic of unique genres: they pervade the melody, the bass and the harmony, strangely matched by the tone of the flute and violin. The similarities between the Sonata and certain *à la mode* chamber works by Zelenka in Dresden or Quantz in Potsdam do not lessen its rich density or its many imaginative turns of phrase.

The king's presentation copy includes three Latin inscriptions, presumably the composer's work: an acrostic on the word 'ricercar' and laudatory tags to two canons. How obsequious or merely polite these

---

[3] The common-property formulas in the theme are: a tonic triad plus diminished seventh; then a descending chromatic fourth; a Neapolitan sixth; and a perfect cadence. The Ricercar à 3 does its best to create a canon *in diminutione*.

are is now unfathomable, but they show a composer sensitive to appropriate allusion (the Sonata uses ordinary Italian, the canons and ricercars a less simple and epigrammatic Latin) and also willing to use music for a message. Thus, as one of the canons modulates upwards a whole tone on each statement and so passes through an octave, 'so may the king's glory rise'. A modulating canon is so unusual as to suggest that the composer planned it explicitly as an allegory.

The Obituary does not repeat the newspaper's report that on the following day, a Monday, Bach played the organ in the Heiligegeistkirche, Potsdam, built for the new church (1730 by Joachim Wagner. Such a pair of performances, at court and church, closely matches Bach's appearances at Dresden, and no doubt he played other organs in Berlin and/or Potsdam, including the Garrison Church, where Wagner had contrived some moving statuary in the organ case to represent the Prussian eagle rising to face the sun. What was played to the large number of listeners is not known, but in addition to improvisations one can suppose a programme of transcriptions and chorale variations, with a prelude to start and fugue to finish. On which Berlin visit it was that Emanuel accompanied his father to see the new opera house on Unter den Linden is uncertain.

[In Leipzig] seldom did he have the luck to find only such performers as would have spared him these irksome comments.

'These irksome comments' are the composer's, mentioned by the Obituary when it claimed he had so fine an ear that even in the fullest ensemble music he could discern the smallest error. The Obituary is contrasting its subject's abilities – his unparalleled gifts of hearing, grasp of harmony and melody, seriousness of purpose, technical and musical mastery of keyboards and their music – with the mundane circumstances in which he found himself.

Traditionally, the Leipzig cantatas have been thought to draw on twelve or sixteen singers SATB and some eighteen instrumentalists, with a total number seldom if ever above forty even on special occasions, and often a good deal fewer. In recent decades, arguments for a yet smaller choir, even one to a part, have often been assembled, though without always distinguishing between types of cantata or quite answering the questions that arise: why could not a single copy of a part be used by three or even more singers, why would they need written cues, how many students were added to the regular performances, what was the situation for Bach's predecessor and successors, when is circumstantial evidence real evidence? After all, there is a clear musical difference between choral and solo writing. Do we even know that the extant voice parts were those used for performance, and if so, were there never any others? And what are we to suppose when extant parts have uncorrected errors, especially in the later cantatas and the 1736 parts for the *St Matthew Passion*?

A little help in understanding cantata performances in general and the cantor's life in particular is provided by two documents of 1730: a memorandum to the town council (the *Entwurf*, of 23 August) expressing grievances over present conditions, and the letter to his childhood friend Georg Erdmann in Danzig (28 October) expressing interest in another post. The first makes it clear that the SATB should have at least two and better three to a part, plus a further soloist for each voice; and since choirs of various standards are needed for the four churches, some thirty-six singers *in toto* are required, plus eighteen or preferably twenty instrumentalists. But there has been a serious shortfall, and he finds only seventeen usable singers and seven instrumentalists. Furthermore, because 'artistry has risen a great deal' since the time of his predecessor Kuhnau ('die Kunst um sehr viel gestiegen'), musicians must now be appointed who are 'suitable for the current musical taste' ('den itzigen musicalischen gustum assequiren': Dok I, p. 63). This last point relates to the increased demands of Bach's full-scale cantatas, with their taxing choral counterpoint and solo arias.

Some exasperation and, one suspects, exaggeration can be read into this document, and it is striking that nothing is said about the boys who lived not in the Thomas School but at home, some of whom would participate in performances. From the time of Arnstadt onwards, he is on

record as finding performers he worked with 'imperfect' ('imperfectis':
Dok II, p. 17), but in 1709 and 1717 his predecessor had also grumbled at
the 'wretched performance' he had been able to achieve, even in carefully prepared works ('elende Execution': Glöckner 2002, pp. 392f.).
Whether anything in particular prompted Bach's new grievances is
unclear. Perhaps they had been building up since a performance of
St Matthew Passion in 1729; perhaps a request to him the day before for
a council election cantata was the last straw. The grievances were an
attacking response to the council's earlier complaints about his con-
tribution to teaching in the school (see below, p. 179), and it is clear
that what he has in view is better circumstances generally – and better
appreciation? – for his music.

How far the renovations to the school building from May 1731 were
one consequence of the aired grievances is not known. The impression
given by various bits of evidence is that Bach had overrated the potential
of the Leipzig situation, that he was not going to achieve a capellmeister's authority there, and that – as his predecessor had implied – the
city's performers and the church's choristers were never going to be
able to give him what he wanted for his complex music. Perhaps the
minor role played by the choir in some cantatas of 1726 indicates that
by then Bach was putting his trust in four solo singers.

The letter to Erdmann also expresses more personal grievances: his
income is not as high as he was led to believe, Leipzig is twice as expensive as other places he has lived in, the authorities are 'strange and
little devoted to music' ('wunderliche und der Music wenig ergebene
Obrigkeit'), and altogether he is subjected to endless 'annoyance, envy
and persecution' ('Verdruß, Neid und Verfolgung': *Dok* I, p. 67). Perhaps Erdmann would speak for him if there were a suitable position in
Danzig? This request is puzzling, for the Baltic cities were musically in
decline and Danzig was no equivalent to Telemann's Hamburg, even
though its chief church of St Mary (with a fine organ) was likely to need
a new capellmeister soon. Perhaps he had learnt of the likely vacancy
and was accustomed to solicit in this way, and the letter to Erdmann

gives a glimpse of normal practice. But a lengthy visit to Dresden a year later, including an appearance at court, was more promising in respect to professional advancement, and was surely intended to be so.

Several things in this appeal to Erdmann, one of the very few extant personal letters written by Bach, are difficult to gauge. That Leipzig was expensive, particularly as it grew over the years 1700–50 from a population of 20,000 to 32,000, is likely. The 'annoyance' he reports is also credible, something he often experienced in various connections with church and school, or at least with their personnel. But 'envy' and 'persecution'? Neither is easy to substantiate from given records and could well indicate how Bach took resistance or discouragement from colleagues, employers and downright philistines. Also hard to evaluate are his seemingly tactless reference to the drop in the number of funerals (and the fees they brought in) when the weather was good, and the description of his family's musical ensemble, with his children all being 'born musicians' ('gebohrne Musici'). Was the first something often discussed between organists, or a sign of pettiness? Was the second a show of fatherly pride or advertisement of the collateral assets of a job-seeker?

Another apparently graceless, if trivial, moment appears in another letter, concerning not music but a barrel of wine sent by his former secretary Johann Elias in 1748. At disproportionate length – perhaps as a joke – Bach describes how it had been damaged, that he cannot yet make an adequate return for it (a gift? a payment?), and that all the taxes and costs he has to pay on such imported liquor make it too expensive a gift (Dok I, p. 119). This is to a cousin from whom he had recently asked a thaler for a copy of the Musical Offering or part of it, having just told him that he had given away gratis to good friends most of the hundred copies he had had engraved (Dok I, p. 117). One hopes the thaler was for postage and that 'good friends' meant potential patrons.

Curiously, the Obituary makes no mention of another ensemble, the Leipzig Collegium Musicum. Yet the last two items in its list of un-published works are 'Various concertos for one, two, three and four harpsichords' and 'a crowd of other instrumental pieces of all sorts and for all kinds of instruments', any of which might have been heard there. Of the Obituary authors, at least Emanuel must have been familiar with the Collegium and its new harpsichord of June 1733, the period when Friedemann was away seeking a position in Dresden and just before Emanuel did likewise in Naumburg. That their father probably participated little in the Collegium concerts after about 1741 may account for the Obituary's silence, though more likely is that a new concert series from 1743, the Grosse Concert, similar to subscription series elsewhere in Europe, had replaced them in the Leipzig public's awareness. While, as already suggested, the Grosse Concert series could have included Passion performances during Lent, like Handel's contemporary Lenten oratorios in London theatres, Bach's participation in them is not recorded, nor is his reaction to any of the new Italian symphonies creeping into concerts generally. It rather looks as if he was (as we might now say) out of the loop.

The earlier private or family music making also fails to feature in accounts, even when Forkel later asked Emanuel for further information on his father's life and works. Yet from details told *en passant* by Emanuel, such as that in Leipzig his father was visited by the Dresden flute virtuoso P.-G. Buffardin, or that he knew very well how to arrange a large orchestra in the open air (Dok III, pp. 287, 288), a glimpse is given of a varied musical life. The Obituary's virtual silence on activities in Leipzig beyond what is implied by the worklist and general remarks means no clue given as to how important to Bach was his concert life. But enough concertos and chamber sonatas exist in a variety of sources – less well organised or conserved than for church music – to suggest that it was far more than an occasional solace.

As he often maintained with regret, it never could come about that he would have a really large and really fine organ for his constant use.

In particular, this remark must reflect the state, size and tone of the organs in the Weimar Chapel (two manuals, about twenty-four stops) and St Thomas's, Leipzig (three manuals, about thirty-five stops).

That both needed wide-ranging work on them while Bach was *titulaire* was nothing out of the ordinary, though his colleagues on the new Silbermann organs in Freiberg or Dresden had no such needs. Silbermann made a point of not rebuilding organs, but the Thomaskirche organ's manuals and pedal combined the work of at least three distinct periods (1598, 1670, 1721) and had to be thoroughly rebuilt again in the 1750s. Perhaps Bach had been agitating in the 1740s for a new organ, hence the Obituary's remark?

The Leipzig university church, or Paulinerkirche, had a large forty-eight-stop three-manual organ by J. Scheibe (the organ tested by Bach in 1717) which in theory could have appropriately realised the great organ works of the Leipzig period, such as *Clavierübung* III and the masterly praeludia in B minor, E minor and C major (9/8), as it could also have been the instrument on which Bach taught pupils. Whether with the phrase 'constant use' the Obituary was referring to this organ, which cannot have been at the cantor's daily disposal, or whether indeed it was fine enough to be an exception to the criticism, is not known. One can read from Bach's report of 1717 either that it was a very good instrument or that it was not, and the latter is likelier.[4]

Without doubt, such a composer and performer had more interest and pleasure in playing organs in the vicinity of Arnstadt, Weimar, Leipzig and Dresden than is now known from various documented visits. Two exceptionally fine instruments in Rötha, for example, would have pleased any visitor, as they still do, and the impression given by books of organ stoplists published by Niedt (1721), Adlung (1768) and others is that organists, as now, had an enthusiastic curiosity about them. The charming early instrument in Pomssen (c1600, also near Leipzig) still has tonal qualities probably like those of the second, older and smaller organ in St Thomas's, which was hanging on the east wall of the nave, above or to the side of the tower arch, facing the

---

[4] The recently built organ in St Thomas's, based on this Scheibe organ for its casework and stoplist, is not , I think, the final answer to the question of a 'Leipzig Bach Organ', being arguably undistinguished in tone, less than handsome and in the wrong place.

cantata performers in the west gallery across the length of the nave. This is the organ one is tempted to think might have played the chorale melody at the beginning of the St Matthew Passion, creating a special stereophony. But it was taken down in 1740, whether to the cantor's annoyance, approval or indifference is not known. There is no evidence that J. S. Bach cared much about preserving old instruments, and if he was responsible for the upkeep of the little organ as he was for the large, its demolition does rather reflect on him.

Nor is it known whether he ever pressed for a Silbermann organ for St Thomas's, although at Zwickau in 1737 his pupil J. L. Krebs had apparently done exactly that very soon after taking up his appointment. Silbermann's tuning would not have suited all of Clavierübung III, nor was he fond of coarse sub-suboctave bass pipes or bright mixture stops of the older type, both of which Bach would probably have wanted, to judge by the priorities he showed at Mühlhausen. On the other hand, Bach's taste for certain classical French music would have been well served by a larger Silbermann organ. It looks very much as if the two men, though apparently on good collegial terms at the Naumburg organ examination of 1746, would have had a personality clash: Silbermann, prone to litigation, had a notion of what an organ was and did not care to change it.

The Obituary says nothing about Bach's interest in other keyboards, this being a much less public matter than organs, and only from incidental references can one build a picture of his involvement with the day's range of stringed keyboards: the four-octave harpsichord of his youth, then the larger single-manual harpsichord, the two-manual harpsichord increasingly popular from c1725, various experimental harpsichords with suboctave strings,[5] the clavichord, the double clavichord and/or harpsichord with independent pedals, the Lautenwerk (small, with two sets of gut strings to imitate a lute), the Gambenwerk (probably

---

[5] It is no more than a guess that the new harpsichord for the Collegium, made by Hildebrandt, had suboctave strings: its cost of 120 reichsthaler (Dähnert 1962, p. 231) was not much above average for a standard single-manual.

with a wheel 'bowing' the strings) and eventually the fortepiano. Several points can be made.

First, there are many early keyboard works such as the Sonata in D major and the *Aria variata* that seem to allow options: if a pedal is available, of whatever type on whatever instrument, it can take certain bass notes; if not, the score can easily be adapted. Like organs, most Thuringian harpsichords of c1700 had a compass of only four octaves, C-c''', so one cannot distinguish between their music on grounds of compass, as some writers have tried to do. But both composers and builders looked increasingly beyond this narrow compass, probably the builders earlier or more adventurously than the composers.

Secondly, during the composer's lifetime there was a gradual move towards specific instrumentation, with music becoming less and less interchangeable. Works became specific or exclusive to the two-manual harpsichord or to the fortepiano or to the full-sized organ. While versatility did not and could not entirely disappear, each repertory increasingly required its instrument to do things another could not. One sees this in Parts I, II and III of the *Clavierübung*: they first require a one-manual harpsichord, then a two-manual, then the organ with two and optionally three manuals.

Thirdly, some instruments must have been 'workhorses', in some sense substitutes for 'full-dress' instruments, and used for practical purposes. Hence the clavichord, which, despite enthusiastic claims now made for it, could be best likened to the upright piano in Victorian homes or school practice rooms. When a Leipzig city clerk taking an inventory of the late capellmeister Bach's possessions in November 1750 called one item '3. *Clavire* nebst *Pedal*' (an instrument that went to the youngest son, Johann Christian: *Dok* II, p. 504), he probably meant a double clavichord – two separate instruments, one placed above the other – plus a third bass clavichord for the pedals. This would have been rather different, one imagines, from the sweet-tongued, long-compass clavichords of the later eighteenth century that substituted for fortepianos and were admired, for some reason, by Emanuel Bach.

Fourthly, incidental references give important hints about the part played by various keyboard instruments. Thus the new harpsichords for the Cöthen court or the Leipzig Collegium were likely to have been far grander than those located in the churches of St Thomas and St Nicholas. The latter were probably intended for rehearsals and not for performance during the service, any more than a piano located in an Anglican cathedral plays in the service anthems or psalms. That Bach was involved in the buying of a *Lautenwerk* in Weimar in 1715, built by his cousin Johann Nicolaus Bach of Jena, is probable, considering reports that he also had one made both while he was in Cöthen and again in Leipzig (*Dok* III, p. 195). Two *Lautenwerke* were listed amongst the deceased composer's possessions, in addition to a veneered harpsichord, three other harpsichords ('Clavesins'), a smaller one, eleven string instruments (including a 'Bassettgen' – violoncello piccolo?) and a spinet (rectangular or bentside? *Dok* II, pp. 492–3). Perhaps the little 'Clavesin' was a simple clavichord, while Johann Christian's '3. Clavire' had been the family's practice instrument for organ music.

Although Bach's inventory might seem rich, no house organ is listed, nor a fortepiano. The rest broadly reflects what was customary amongst German organists, who showed less interest in or knowledge of fine harpsichords than their English or French colleagues. (As well as a house organ, Handel in London possessed two fine seventeenth-century Flemish harpsichords, but no other keyboards are mentioned: *HHB*, p. 441.) What the advantage of the *Lautenwerk* was other than a pretty sound is unclear: easier to tune or voice or restring, less sensitive to climate, less loud, good for accompanying? Also unknown is whether Bach showed an interest in contemporary developments of the clavichord – Silbermann's *cembalo d'amour* with double-length strings, for example, or the dulcimer stop imitating Hebenstreit's *pantaleon*, a large hammered dulcimer much admired at the Dresden court. Yet both men were in his circle of acquaintance: Emanuel owned a Silbermann clavichord (see the Rondo Wq 66), and Friedemann's appointment at the Dresden Sophienkirche in 1733 was supported by Hebenstreit, who had authority for the court's Protestant music.

> His serious temperament drew him predominantly to
> hard-working [*arbeitsamen*], serious and profound music; but he
> could also, if it seemed necessary, particularly when playing,
> make himself comfortable with a light and jocular manner
> of thinking.

This is a key observation in the Obituary, and can be usefully considered in its two parts, which are not contradictory.

The first part suggests that already the aura of the serious attached itself to the image of J. S. Bach. That is also the picture literally drawn by the extant portraits of him, actual images that remain to this day in the minds of his listeners. But an aura of the serious is found in the portraits of other men of the time, especially those with imperfect eyesight. It does not imply that the 'hard work' involved in composing a Brandenburg Concerto, or the way its counterpoint 'works so hard', leads to something gloomy, studious, humourless. On the contrary. It is important now to understand the kind of piety with which a Lutheran orphan was inculcated: the grateful reverence that could make Bach write 'J. J.' ('Jesu juva', 'Jesus, help') on any sort of music, whether a set of harpsichord concertos for the concert room or a set of chorale preludes for church.[6] I would understand this piety in the following way.

As one of God's creatures who had been taught the Gospel's parable of the talents, Bach had been endowed with a gift, exceptional (how conscious was he of this?) but nevertheless something to be returned daily to his Maker, increased by hard work. To return the gift with interest meant not only conscientious self-application but also a deeper commitment, the offering to his Maker of everything he could create through the talent he had been given: simple or complex music, beautiful melody or rich harmony, exciting rhythms or calm counterpoint, appropriate word setting, biblical allusions or dance music, fugues or songs, exercises for himself or others – in short, everything. Reasoning in this way, one can speculate that indeed Bach was at his most pious

---

[6] So in the autograph MSS for both the concerto BWV 1052 and the chorale BWV 651.

11 Portrait of J. S. Bach.
A copy from 1748 by the painter E. G. Haussmann of his original portrait of 1746. The latter, now in Leipzig, shows more substantial signs of later alteration, so the version reproduced here is usefully regarded as the most true-to-life picture of J. S. Bach at about the age of sixty. The music is the 'triple canon' BWV 1076, also published by the composer as a separate print, communicated by him to members of Mizler's Corresponding Society in 1747 and included in the Fourteen Canons he added by hand to his own copy of the Goldberg Variations.

not when the music most moved or delighted his neighbour but when it was so complex or thoughtfully wrought as to be understood only by himself and his Maker. He returned his God-given talent with more interest the farther he developed it.

Obscurity or complexity would not be a virtue in itself, for, music being music, the result could become turgid, over-rhetorical, even tiresome, in one way or another the consequence of vainglory or insolence. But for the God-given talent to be developed, stretched as far as a mere mortal could stretch it, new paths of contrapuntal ingenuity or formal organisation must be taken. All is devotional for the devout man, and 'with a music that is devotional, God is always present in his grace', as Bach wrote in the margin of his house Bible at 2 Chronicles 5:13 (Cox 1985, facsimile 112). These verses in Chronicles describe how voices and instruments were used to praise the Lord, and the marginal note, written in about 1733, is the classic response by a Lutheran (or Anglican) of the time, who found nothing but poor theology in the Calvinist (or Presbyterian) argument against music in or out of church.

Such reasoning could alone explain why at first in Leipzig Bach made a point of supplying a new cantata each week. He did not have to do this, and at other moments in the service he kept the customary music of previous generations, quasi-plainsong intonations, motets, and classic Protestant chorales already two centuries old. In drawing at first on works written at Weimar a few years earlier, his Leipzig cantatas were maintaining the high, one might say aristocratic, tone, adapted somewhat for the new conditions but bringing to a parish church congregation a means of raising their sensibilities to the Word made sound. If the previous repertory (Kuhnau's) was discarded, this cannot have been for reasons simply of modernity: the supererogatory complexity of Bach's audition cantatas of 1723 already foretold a unique repertory, unmatched at the time but seldom modern in any superficial sense. If the wish was simply to be modern, an easier solution was to take the recent works by other Lutheran composers, whole church years of cantatas (Telemann's were soon to be published), simple, tuneful, practical works, at their best up to date. Or he could have imitated such works himself, improving on their harmonic flabbiness and conveying more imaginatively than they the *Affekt* of texts. But seldom if ever would one mistake a Leipzig cantata movement for the work of a Graupner or Telemann, though one might occasionally for the work of another member of the Bach clan.

Complexity of musical thought takes many forms, and it looks as if especially in his last dozen years Bach had in mind, when composing in some particular genre, a carefully made list of the ways in which he could expose the intricacies of God's gift of music. In *Clavierübung* III, a modern trio sonata (as if for flute, violin and continuo) is heard against an old Lutheran chorale melody played in canon, twice; both settings speak a remote musical dialect and are unique in their different ways as settings of the Lord's Prayer and Ten Commandments chorales. A series of canons in the Goldberg Variations is set within the almost intolerably narrow confines of a few common-property harmonies; the variations begin without upbeats – a further challenge, as if another act of supererogation – and hover in a world of uncanny sound never otherwise heard. A series of fugues and canons in the *Art of Fugue*, derived from a quasi-antique theme, demonstrates ways in which both theme and structure can be treated. All of these works are supplying actual *exempla* of musical *teoria*, but in the process create an otherwise unknown world of beautiful sound.

The complex late works of Bach imply that in addition to the high, middle and low styles (recognised also in the poetry of the period), he had another category in mind: the transcendental. Hence the *Art of Fugue*, perhaps first intended as a further part of the *Clavierübung*, or 'Keyboard Practice'.[7] Its history is uncertain: by c1742, a set of fourteen fugues and two canons based on a single varied theme had been compiled, and this was later added to and published posthumously. It is possible that Bach remembered J.-H. d'Anglebert's *Pièces de clavecin* of 1689, which includes five fugues in D minor on a single varied theme, plus another on three combined subjects (a modest anticipation of Bach's). Whether 'The

---

[7] The Goldberg Variations were called 'Clavierübung', without number.

Art of Fugue' was the composer's title and 'Contrapunctus' his name for the movements are other questions without certain answer. The title was added to the MS by Bach's pupil Altnickol in about 1745, and conforms to fashionable references to 'art' in various writings, including the Obituary. 'Contrapunctus', rather than the usual 'Contrapunct' (German) or 'contrapunctum' (Latin), recalls Buxtehude's memorial publication of 1674 for his own father.

What the composer's intended shape or plan was, if any, is uncertain, both in the extant MS (when variants of the canons already appear) and the engraving (begun a year or two before he died: Dok III, p. 3). Emanuel spoke of twenty-four pieces in the edition, counting each inverted fugue and the final chorale, and this was surely for him an allusive number. Like the Canonic Variations for organ, the Art of Fugue may have had no single authorised form, despite today's surmises about an 'earlier version' (MS) or 'later version' (posthumous print). Together, they have the appearance of a work-in-progress portfolio, one that included arrangements (two fugues rewritten for two harpsichords), revisions (with change of notation), perhaps a completed final fugue and yet other movements. 'Later' readings are not superior to 'earlier'.

Such a portfolio would suggest a composer indefatigably learning and gathering examples, counting off the ways to treat themes, exploring the behaviour of music's notes as a chemist might explore the earth's elements. In both versions, the movements not only increase in contrapuntal complexity, as if laying out a practical study in fugue, but the fugue subject is varied, as if creating another kind of variation form, beyond the Goldbergs, the *Musical Offering* and the Canonic Variations. Each of these solves in its own way the chief problem of ordinary sets of variations (see above, p. 54). One interesting detail is that a movement with jerky 'French' rhythms, headed in the posthumous edition 'in Stylo Francese', comes halfway in the MS compilation, exactly as a Frenchified movement does in each of the four volumes of the *Clavierübung*.

As for the transcendental element, the harpsichord duets of the *Art of Fugue* were first conceived as three-voice fugues in 'correct' form (*forma recta*), then put upside down in the layout and the intervals (*forma inversa*). Their lines move in ways they would not if they did not also have to work upside down, and the ear soon recognises something rich and strange. There is another pair of such fugues, quite different in character, and these four movements are matched by another foursome: a set of canons in two voices, at the octave, tenth (unusual) and twelfth (less so), plus one in which the second voice inverts and doubles the length of the notes of the first. All this ingenuity has a musical purpose, for it results in a harmony recognisable as new and 'unworldly', challenging the logic of conventional harmonic progressions as nothing else can.

The *Art of Fugue* may indeed be an example of the 'hard-working, serious and profound music' of which the Obituary authors were speaking, for it was on their mind as they were writing. And yet, there is much in it that is both exceptionally beautiful and beautifully effortless, simple, direct, with a harmony (like that of the *Orgelbüchlein*) best realised on the keyboard but in principle indifferent to tone colour. Though undoubtedly serious, the opening group of four fugues of the MS version remains some of the sweetest counterpoint ever created by any composer. While Contrapunctus 4 undoubtedly 'introduced a highly innovative modification of the inverted theme' (Wolff 2000, p. 435), it is the sheer sensuality of certain harmony (dominant minor ninths) that is really dazzling. Elsewhere, in the complex play of themes or canons, one has the impression that Bach is answering the initiated listener's question, 'Now how is he going to deal with that little problem?' Yet the harmony of the fugue subject is so reliable that there is no limit to the number of countersubjects. Many a teacher since then will have found that the best-ever fugal creation in a student's career was based on one or other version of the subject of the *Art of Fugue*.

One of the problems peculiar to Bach is that reverence for his masterful counterpoint, together with acute regret for his unfinished projects, diverts attention away from its simple beauty. The reverence due to the *Art of Fugue* was deepened when its editors included an unfinished fugue, copied in late 1749 (?) but left incomplete – because of the composer's illness, according to the Obituary, which also speaks of an even more complex missing fugue, invertible note for note.[8] The print's editors said that to compensate for the incomplete fugue they were adding a chorale 'dictated in his blindness to one of his friends' (Dok III, p. 13). (As in England at the time, 'friends' would include 'relatives', such as a daughter or son-in-law.) But since at least the combination of four themes in the incomplete fugue needed to be worked out beforehand, since it cannot be inverted (this would require a different piece of music), and since, finally, the 'dictated chorale' derives from a much older piece, there is some difficulty in accepting these various claims, all of which generate a required odour of sanctity.

The personal element introduced in the incomplete fugue – bringing in a theme based on the notes B A C H – matches the clear appearance of the same notes at the end of the Canonic Variations in the composer's copy. The two could well be near-contemporary, and suggest that in his maturity he wished to make his mark, as an act of piety, on such complex music. That still leaves a big question about the final fugue: was it finished or not? The extant manuscript's last page was unusable, so was there once another? Or is it possible that, as with another late fugue (in C minor, for organ), the composer lost interest in it? Despite the awesomely ingenious way it harmonises its three themes so far, their relentless exploitation can be found progressively less enthralling.

The second part of the Obituary's observation sounds rather like a defence against accusations: nobody would have accused Handel of being unduly serious. It needed saying, however, to those for whom Bach as composer, player or teacher was the hero of difficult counterpoint rather than the master of dance music and tuneful miniatures, as he also was.

While the Obituary is careful to spread its praise over a wide range of musical abilities, it could certainly have given a fuller picture of the composer by discussing such masterpieces as the Peasant Cantata (1742) – fuller, that is, than merely referring generally to 'some comic vocal

---

[8] The posthumous edition and the Obituary seem confused as to what is incomplete or missing. Note that the extant autograph MS and the print do not break off at the same point.

pieces' ('einige komische Singstücke': *Dok* III, p. 86). From the Peasant Cantata, and to a lesser extant the Coffee Cantata and other non-church pieces, it is tempting to speculate, as over-reverential admiration does not, what comic operas or intermezzi Bach may have been perfectly capable of, had the opportunity been there. The comedy and suggestiveness in such works as the Peasant and Coffee Cantatas are not so far from those in Pergolesi's *La serva padrona* (1733) or even Pepusch's *Beggar's Opera* (1729), for their music not only suits the picaresque but naturally exudes the *double entendre*. When a soprano's elegant melody sighs at the sweetness of coffee, one wonders, 'Is this really only about coffee?'[9]

For both Bach and Picander, the librettist of the Peasant and Coffee Cantatas as well as the *St Matthew Passion*, there was no puritan need to evade the racy in either music or text. Both poet and composer recognised the higher, middle and lower styles, each having its place and deserving professional attention. Only an astonishingly versatile composer could have been writing both the Peasant Cantata and, apparently over the same period, much of the *Art of Fugue*. But idiom varies according to genre, and for a skilful poet or composer there is no problem in having a character in the Peasant Cantata sing 'Let's have a cuddle' and following it with a suggestive little tune in the violins. Or when the characters finally go off to the tavern, trailing the dudelsack like a pied piper, they sing a bourrée that at half the speed and harmonised appropriately would sound like the final chorale of a cantata. As it is, the tone is clearly of a piece with the phallic and pudendal *double entendres* in the Wedding Quodlibet BWV 524 (1707). Anna Magdalena Bach's wedding verses in her album of 1725 are milder but still with *double entendre* as well as *amour tendre*.

Not that one has to be prurient to tease or joke, as can be seen in the tongue-in-cheek formal phraseology with which in 1741 Bach

---

9 At much the same period, in correspondence between Jonathan Swift and his friend Vanessa, coffee served as a code for their encounters, in a 'special sexually charged sense of intimacy' (D. Nokes, *Jonathan Swift: A Hypocrite Reversed*, London, 1985, p. 258).

acknowledges the above-mentioned gift of some venison from a family
friend at the court of Weissenfels, proof of 'Your Honour's invaluable
favour' of which 'I never entertained the faintest doubt', and which
has been 'meanwhile eaten by us to the health of Your Honour' (Dok I,
p. 110). There is also something witty in his quoting one of Luther's
Latin sayings – 'its key will be seen at the end' – in connection with
a certain canon (Dok I, p. 222).[10] Not the least interesting point made
by the Obituary is that it was 'particularly when playing' that Bach was
'comfortable with a light and jocular manner of thinking' ('leichten und
schertzhaften Denkart'). Is this a warning against taking his late learned
publications as representing the whole man? An eye-witness report of
what and how he played in less formal settings? Does 'playing' ('Spiel-
en') mean keyboard music or, more likely, performance in general, as
in the Collegium concerts or at home or in recitals at court? Rather than
'jocular' or 'humorous', 'schertzhaft' could be a synonym for 'allegro',
'light, cheerful, bright': Bach's playing was effortless, bright, uplifting,
the opposite of stodgy.

> We will not be ill thought of if we are so bold as to go on
> asserting that our Bach was the greatest organist and keyboard
> player that we have ever had . . . He had worked out for himself
> such a comfortable fingering that it was not hard for him to
> perform the greatest difficulties with the most fluent ease.
> Before him the best-known keyboard players in Germany and
> other countries had made little use of the thumb.

To want to call him the 'greatest' could well have been responding to
a tendency in biographies of the day to evaluate a composer's practical abilities, as when Mattheson described Handel as 'strong on the
organ, stronger than Kuhnau in fugues and counterpoint, especially
ex tempore' (1740, p. 93). To mention Kuhnau rather than Handel's
teacher Zachow may have been a slip – but did it prompt the Obituary's
praise for Kuhnau's successor? His critic Scheibe, discussed below,

---

[10] This was not unique: G. F. Kauffmann also quotes it in his *Harmonische Seelenlust*,
1733, p. 7, for a chorale that ends on an imperfect cadence.

had also implied in print that Bach's only rival 'as an extraordinary artist on harpsichord and organ' was Handel (Dok II, pp. 286, 300), and so left it necessary for Bach devotees to make a counter-claim, one of several made after his death. During his Leipzig years he had already been praised – in print – as a player, director of the Collegium, a clever composer, and furthermore, one admired in Italy itself (Dok II, p. 469).

Other testimony to the composer's skill as a player refers in general terms both to organ ('I have never heard anything like it', G. H. L. Schwanenberger in 1727: Dok II, p. 179) and to harpsichord (he still admired Froberger suites in later years, according to J. Adlung in 1758: Dok III, p. 124). His violin playing, which he kept up until the approach of old age, was described by Emanuel as 'pure and penetrating' ('rein u. durchdringend': Dok III, p. 285), which looks less than complimentary, except that it meant he could hold an orchestra together better with violin than from the keyboard. He preferred playing viola, 'with appropriate louds and softs', as presumably the usual humble viola player did not when sawing away at his customarily tedious parts. If Bach's preference for viola is correctly reported, perhaps one might stretch this to include the large viola or violoncello piccolo, required in some Weimar and Leipzig cantatas and much better known in mid-century Saxony than is now often recognised.[11]

Bach's singing voice was also 'penetrating', with a wide compass and good technique ('gute Singart': ibid.), qualities which he clearly found reasonable to require of his singers. Various accounts of his imaginative realisation of figured bass as a continuo player were given by pupils, who would have been receptive to a dazzling teacher able so to 'accompany every solo that one thinks it an ensemble piece', with a new melody as if precomposed, according to Lorenz Mizler in 1738 (Dok II, p. 321). Mizler does not ask whether this picture is entirely to the composer's credit, but I doubt that it is, any more than was his egregious realisation of a figured bass by Antonio Biffi many years before (see BJ 1997, p. 12) – if, that

---

[11] Whoever composed the world-famous 'Toccata and Fugue in D minor for organ', it could well have originated as a piece for violoncello piccolo solo, arranged for organ.

is, the realisation is for playing and not merely for studying harmony. It lacks an Italian composer's panache, and if for Bach continuo harmony was as complete as written-out harmony, his pupils could easily have produced the kind of literal, tedious accompaniment published by J. P. Kirnberger for the *Musical Offering*. A teacher's emphasis on careful harmonisation could lead students less gifted than himself to a pedantic and unidiomatic kind of playing.

A report from 1738 of Bach's directing thirty or forty musicians – in a church cantata? – with a nod to one, a foot-tap to another and a warning finger to a third, speaks of his noticing everything at once and holding it all together with 'rhythm in every limb' ('membris omnibus rhythmicum': *Dok* II, p. 232). This is another report in print that could well have been familiar to the Obituary authors, who spoke of his ability to discern errors in an ensemble. Although nothing less would be expected, one begins to suspect again that Emanuel was drawing on a file Bach kept of such cuttings, for himself or for posterity. The Obituary may not distinguish between the composer's youth and maturity, but one can assume that he had always been able to control an ensemble: the image of an all-seeing *director musices* fits in with so many other elements in the picture, including the pleasure he took in anticipating what a fugue composer was going to do with a theme (see below, p. 200). Since this is not so very difficult, was this more than a bit of naive showing-off?

There is a context to the more specific details in the Obituary's second sentence above. Already in his vastly informative and widely selling book of 1752, Emanuel's Berlin colleague J. J. Quantz had spoken not only in general terms of the 'perfection' to which Bach had brought organ playing – presumably he had heard him play, at Potsdam in 1747 or at Dresden in the 1730s – but of his keyboard technique. According to Quantz, each of his fingers was curled and its tip drawn in to glide off the keys, producing fast passages at their clearest, especially scale runs ('stufenweis': 1752, pp. 232, 329). But how far such articulation and touch were characteristic of Bach's earlier playing, especially before the partitas of the late 1720s, is quite uncertain, and Quantz might just as well have had at the back of his mind examples given in Couperin's keyboard tutor, *L'art de toucher*.

Bach's counterpoint, however, does require careful, cohesive fingering. Hence it is that the title page of the Inventions of 1723 speaks of players learning from them 'above all, to achieve a singing style in the playing' ('am allermeisten aber eine *cantable* Art im Spielen zu erlangen': Dok I, p. 221). This 'cantab[i]le' is not Chopin's but Couperin's: the smooth harpsichord line already implied in *L'art de toucher* but especially necessary in fugal counterpoint. That Bach, however, like all the best keyboard composers of the time, wanted variety of touch is suggested by adjacent pieces in the set of Inventions: the fully slurred D major Invention supposes a quite different playing style from the slurless D minor Invention that follows. Such variety had to be learnt, and in this as in other respects Bach's early music must have differed from his later in playing style: it is hard to believe that the *Aria variata* of c1705 and the Goldberg Variations of thirty-five years later required the same kind of fingering and articulation. The instrument's sound production and the very keyboard itself had evolved towards making greater smoothness and sensitive touch possible, and so must have its playing.

In his book of 1753, Emanuel implies that his father had gradually developed the way of using the thumb and making all fingers versatile – for the sake of playing in all twenty-four keys? – and had told him of hearing in his youth great men who used the thumb only for wide stretches, not for scales or remoter keys (Dok III, p. 23). This recalls Quantz's reference to 'the Netherlanders' of former times, for both he and Emanuel may be referring obliquely to Reinken and Buxtehude, whose fingering was doubtless less versatile, since organ tuning allowed fewer keys, composers wrote harmony with fewer sevenths and modulations, and even the keyboard's sharps and naturals were shorter. Or Quantz may have had in mind Mattheson's recent praise for the long-dead but still admired Amsterdam organist Sweelinck, and his 'pleasant and decorous' way of playing the keyboard ('angenehm und ehrbar': 1740, under 'Jacob Praetorius').

In his own book, Emanuel says that he is now using this 'new finger-ing' as the foundation of his own Method, which catered for music very different from his father's. Whether the Obituary's remark on finger-ing predates these books by Quantz and Emanuel Bach is uncertain, for though apparently it was ready before they were published (see *Dok* III, p. 7), what exactly it contained is not known. But a much earlier book, very likely known to Emanuel, had advised that

> To produce a fast run more continuous than that in [the given musical example], it is only a matter of becoming accustomed to passing the thumb under whatever finger one wishes, and to passing one of the other fingers over the thumb.

> Pour continuer un roulement plus étendu que celui de la Leçon, il n'y a qu'à s'accoutumer à passer le I. par-dessous tel autre doigt que l'on veut, & à passer l'un de ces autres doigts par-dessus le I.

Although Rameau's *Pièces de clavecin avec une méthode sur la mécanique des doigts* (Paris, 1724) is not known to have been owned by either Bach, one might guess that it was and that it had had a crucial influence on the harpsichord partitas, above all because of the sheer quality and subtle modernity of Rameau's music, which was more than a rival to Handel's suites of 1720. Rameau required flexible fingering and flexible use of the hands, including left-hand-over – as in the Gigue of Bach's first partita (1726). Bach's skill with hand-crossing and wide leaps was actually praised by his critic Johann Scheibe (*Dok* II, p. 286, see below).

While Emanuel's and Rameau's treatments of fingering do not en-tirely coincide – for example, Emanuel uses the little finger 5 more, on sharps and flats – nevertheless to read especially paragraphs 7, 11, 18, 22, 25–7, 33 and 61 in the first chapter of Emanuel's book alongside Rameau's *Pièces* of 1724 is to be struck by similarities. It looks very much as if Emanuel is aiming for the coherence and comprehensiveness lack-ing (promised but never fulfilled) in the brief remarks of Rameau, an author whom the *Versuch* mentions only once, and then to criticise. Is the Obituary's phrase 'keyboardists [*Clavieristen*] of other countries' less a reference to the Netherlands than an attempt to demote French publications by claiming Bach's precedence?

As far as his father's music is concerned, one can take Emanuel's remarks as relevant at best only to the mature Leipzig keyboard works. Since J. S. Bach's earlier years, many things had changed: pitch was generally lower, temperament less unequal, instruments' sound production less immediate, keyboards had longer keys and compass, counterpoint was better wrought. As repertory had changed, so had playing, even in technical details such as ornaments. The ornament table in Friedemann's *Clavierbüchlein* (1720), which is derived from much older French models, can say little for the *Musical Offering* (1747). As for fingering, thumbs on any sharp and finger substitution on any note are both important in such counterpoint as that of the *Art of Fugue* (1740s), if the integrity of the counterpoint is to be observed. All this means that the player today justifiably doubts whether the writings of c1750 say much about the music of c1710.

He understood not only the art of playing organs, uniting together their stops in the most skilful way and letting each stop be heard in its true character, all to the greatest perfection: he also knew from first to last how organs were constructed. [One organ he examined was at the Johanniskirche, Leipzig] near to where his bones now rest. The maker was a man in the final years of his old age, and the examination was perhaps one of the severest that had ever been made. Consequently, the full approval that our Bach publicly conferred on the organ directed no little honour as much to the organ builder as also, on account of certain circumstances, to Bach himself.

This reference contains at least three motifs important to a Bach biography.

First, the claims that he had a deep technical knowledge of organs, both as to how they could sound well and as to how they were constructed. Neither is difficult to believe, but only in general terms. They go with the picture drawn by Emanuel that he understood the physical layout of orchestras as well as organs, even orchestras placed in the open air, and that he once recognised how a certain building (the banqueting hall of the new Berlin opera house) could produce an unintended and so far unnoticed whispering-gallery effect. All this was achieved through experience and 'natural' knowledge, not through a 'systematic study of acoustics' (Dok III, pp. 285, 288). Hard though it is to believe that a whispering-gallery effect would have gone unnoticed in a building several years old, Emanuel found it important to claim that nature and practice, not theory or system, could account for his father's observation.

As for the use of organ stops, organists of that time and place must have been familiar with G. F. Kauffmann's set of chorales published in Leipzig in the 1730s, which included detailed stop registrations for large organs, and they could well have been puzzled why Bach's collections did not. *Clavierübung* III, the Canonic Variations and the Schübler Chorales (all from between c1738 and c1748) indicate nothing beyond the manuals and octave pitch required, and then not completely. Kauffmann was not alone in indicating the stops, and indeed, not to do so at all was somewhat old-fashioned – more typical of an organ culture in which music had only circulated in manuscript and where each region's organs varied only according to size. To publish complex music without specifying stops drew attention to the counterpoint *per se* rather than to its performance, and this could well have been Bach's intention. But the Obituary authors then covered the registration issue by claiming Bach's unrivalled mastery of it.

Some consideration has already been given to Bach's supposedly intimate understanding of organ building (see above, p. 41). Quite why the Obituary authors would claim that Bach understood the structural technicalities of organs is not obvious. Because it was true? Or because by then such expertise was exceptional? Or was it that not being experts themselves, they overstated his expertise? From the anecdote about the whispering-gallery effect in Berlin it seems that evidence is seldom straightfoward, for this report bears a curious resemblance to one about an 'echo tower' in Weimar (see Wolff 2000, p. 506), which somebody – father or son? – could have known. In the case of the rebuilding scheme for the Mühlhausen organ, one can point out that it had much in common not only with Werckmeister's book but also with Christoph Bach's improvement plan of 1696 for the organ in St George's, Eisenach. And as for any particular taste J. S. Bach had for strong bass tone, with ample wind to supply it, other schemes of the period show that this was quite typical of Thuringian organists, though less so of those in Hamburg or Dresden. One could say something similar about Bach's other preferences in organ building, as implied by various other bits of evidence: nothing suggests that they differed much from provincial tastes in 1700 or so.

The second motif in the Obituary's remarks was capellmeister Bach's generosity to craftsmen, a detail developed by Emanuel in later remarks to Forkel. But if they thought it was unusual for examiners to ask for supplementary payment for an organ builder they cannot have read Werckmeister's *Orgelprobe* very carefully, for he recommends it. It is doubtful that Emanuel had read it. Besides, the town council itself recognised that the builder Johann Scheibe was 'a poor man' (*Dok* II, p. 408), and had probably been willing to help him. The strictness of the Johanniskirche examination was mentioned again later by Adlung (*Dok* III, p. 192), presumably drawing on the Bach Obituary, but considering how relatively modest an instrument of two manuals and twenty-two stops is, a long and rigorous examination could well mean that there were problems with it.

The third motif in the Obituary's remarks is hidden in the coy little phrase 'on account of certain circumstances', for without doubt this refers to the notorious criticism of Bach levelled in 1737 by none other than the organ builder's son, J. A. Scheibe, a former student of Bach in Leipzig. (Neither church nor builder is specified by the Obituary, despite Bach's being buried in the Johanniskirche. Scheibe Sr was sixty-five in 1743 when the examination was made, and his son's critique was probably still fresh at that time.) If Bach was fair to the father, irrespective of his son's notorious criticism, does this suggest that from experience the Obituary authors expected otherwise? A striking point about the reference is that it is the only one in the whole Obituary that even hints at Bach's various quarrels and vexations, and some attention can now be given to it.

It was in Hamburg in May 1737, in the journal *Der critische Musikus*, that J. A. Scheibe, unsuccessful candidate at the Leipzig Nikolaikirche in 1729 (where Bach had been examiner), accused Bach's music of the following (Dok II, pp. 286ff.):

having insufficient 'agreeableness' ('Annehmlichkeit') when compared to 'a great master of music in a foreign country'

discarding nature ('das Natürliche entzöge') with a turgid and confused manner ('schwülstiges', 'verworrenes')

obscuring beauty by too much art ('allzu grosse Kunst')

requiring singers and instrumentalists to do what he alone can do on the keyboard

writing out every little embellishment, covering over the melody and removing the beauty of harmony

making the voice parts equally difficult (i.e. contrapuntal, none of them a soloist or *Hauptstimme*)

all achieved with heavy labour ('beschwerliche Arbeit').

Presumably it was Bach himself who got J. A. Birnbaum, a Leipzig teacher of rhetoric, to defend him several times at length against the absent Scheibe. Having someone else to reply when his activities had been questioned seems also to be the case at Naumburg in 1746, when the organist challenged Bach's and Silbermann's positive report on the new organ: only the latter is known to have responded (Dok II, pp. 429–31). And in 1749, when the rector in Freiberg, Saxony, published a somewhat anti-music document, Bach asked C. G. Schröter, a much-respected organist and one of his defenders against Scheibe, to respond. On this occasion Bach's opinion was more intolerantly and rudely expressed than Schröter liked, and it gave Mattheson, who got to know about it, a chance to poke his nose in and offer gratuitous comment (Dok II, p. 462).

Bach must have supplied some of Birnbaum's arguments for the defence, though surely not their long-winded expression. They include the following, here paraphrased (Dok II, pp. 296ff.):

Bach deserves to be called more than *Musicant* or *Künstler* (musician, artist), since these imply mere practitioners or craftsmen.

If Handel is the 'great master in a foreign country' able to dispute the palm with Bach, others think him no equal.

There is a misunderstanding about *Annehmlichkeit*: music is more than merely agreeable sounds, as Joseph Addison points out in the London *Spectator*.

Schwülstiges is an indiscriminate charge, but Bach's decorations are appropriate to the genre in hand.

Verworrenes is precisely what his counterpoint is not, though Scheibe might have heard confused performances (of Leipzig cantatas?).

Allzu grosse Kunst cannot destroy nature or obscure beauty. By definition, any difficulty in playing is surmountable: as the Dresden orchestra shows, accuracy of ensemble is perfectly possible (another hint of Leipzig imperfections and of Dresden as the ideal?).

Many another music prescribes ornaments, as in the organ works of Grigny and Du Mage. To specify them sensibly conveys a composer's intentions.

To have no 'solo line' is not a fault: Palestrina and Lotti did not either.

Aware that he was not able always to call on virtuoso performers, Bach was able to adapt his music accordingly.

A few more replies and counter-replies were made, and yet several of Scheibe's points were not very well answered. Invoking Palestrina or Grigny does not really bear on his points, which were less against counterpoint or ornament signs as such than against superfluous complexity. He was clearly thinking of works in which Handel's simple melodiousness is missing, or in which melodies are so cluttered with busy figuration as to deprive soloists of their usual freedoms. Perhaps Scheibe is also implying that the choir and musicians of St Thomas's found the music too hard, which he would know from personal experience. Indeed, several of his points suggest by no means merely philosophical differences in taste but actual experience of the problems with some of Bach's vocal and instrumental writing, specifically church cantatas.

Scheibe's points were not merely those of a Hamburg musician by now more at home with the easier music of a Telemann or Handel, nor do they become worthless if his opinions were not his own, as Schröter already suspected (*Dok* II, p. 433). For much of what he says rings true. Surely the most ardent Bach devotees can become aware sometimes of 'too much art' and find their own examples when this has seemed to be the case: the teeth-gritting dogma of the F major duet of the *Clavierübung* or of the Augmentation Canon of the *Art of Fugue*; the sheer thoroughness of twice collecting preludes and fugues in every major and minor key (so entrenched has the *Well-Tempered Clavier* become that one easily forgets how strange it is); the earnest calculation in early Leipzig cantata choruses and arias; the hard work represented by all his collections, whose very variety can be somehow distancing. Given that in the 1730s, in the early stages of the German Enlightenment, views differed on what was 'natural', as they must and still do, Scheibe would understandably find Bach's music too often the product of heavy labour and therefore less 'natural' than Handel's.

Rivalry with Handel in the minds of the Obituary authors reached its apogee in the 1788 *Comparison of Bach and Handel*, probably written by C. P. E. Bach (*Dok* III, pp. 437–45). Part of the picture in the *Comparison*, authentic or not, was of his father's abortive attempts to meet Handel in person, whose departures from Halle would doubtless remind readers of Marchand's departure from Dresden. But Scheibe's appreciation of Handel did not mean demeaning Bach: in 1745 he warmly praised the Italian Concerto in F major for harpsichord, calling it a 'perfect model of a well-organised concerto for one player' ('vollkommenes Muster eines wohleingerichteten einstimmigen Concerts', *Dok* II, p. 373), as indeed it is. The Italian Concerto has much of the light touch typical of Italian concertos and shows an intimate awareness of how such pieces could be. But it is also much more carefully thought-out than his models, and planned so precisely that the three movements have a common pulse and proportional time signatures. Also, it has an affecting slow movement full of written-out ornamentation, just such as Scheibe originally criticised; it is technically demanding, as if the composer expected other players to be able 'to do what he alone can do on the keyboard'; and it is throughout far less 'natural' in its melodies than other music of the 1730s. Nevertheless, Scheibe found it agreeable and so proved himself able to discriminate between degrees of acceptability.

It is likely that Scheibe's original criticism not only expressed a general idea of 'nature' then fashionable – a buzzword of the Enlightenment period and of Leipzig poets such as his teacher Gottsched – but also reflected Gottsched's displeasure some years previously at finding his notions mocked, or so it has been thought, in Bach's inspired cantata 'Phoebus and Pan' (1729).[12] On the whole, though, there seems little need to invoke philosophical, highfalutin ideas of the natural when looking at Scheibe's criticisms: if one compares Handel's 'My heart is inditing' for the coronation of George II in October 1727 with Bach's Cantata 198 of the same month on the death of the Electress of Saxony, one can see what Scheibe meant and how he would feel his opinions to be totally justified. For however richly and undeniably beautiful to the connoisseur much of Cantata 198 might be, 'My heart is inditing' (likewise for a queen consort) is more immediately winsome and, to more people, natural. The Obituary authors were well aware how often Scheibe and Mizler had praised Handel in various publications of the 1730s and 1740s.

Against the background of Scheibe's criticisms, one might also consider the B minor Mass. The first two movements sent to the newly installed Elector of Saxony in July 1733 had been appropriate both to the Protestant congregation in and around the court – a Lutheran *missa* of two movements – and to the Roman Catholic royal family. The longer,

---

[12] Or perhaps this is a conjecture too far, since Bach was to use a Gottsched libretto in 1738 for a Collegium performance of the cantata BWV Anh. I 13. But quarrels and quasi-reconciliations are not unknown in university communities.

modishly Italianate masses by the court's composer J. D. Zelenka gave some precedent for a completed mass of many full-scale movements when Bach worked further during his final years to finish his own. This composition of the Credo, Sanctus, Benedictus and Agnus Dei – both their supposedly new and their rewritten movements – speak for Bach's endless creativity, whether or not he had a particular purpose in mind for the finished B minor Mass. No such purpose is documented, nor is any actual performance during his lifetime, but the greater his disappointment with Leipzig, the likelier that a full mass would have been intended for Dresden, for the royal *cappella* and even for its new church then under construction, the Catholic Court Chapel.

Silbermann's organ for this new but delayed church was completed only after his death in 1754, which means that neither of two out-standing masterpieces of late Baroque art in Saxony – Bach's mass and Silbermann's three-manual organ – was heard as intended by its creator. Just as Silbermann kept traditional organ sounds but added a few stops required by the tastes of the day – a Chalumeau, a céleste – so Bach kept to traditional counterpoint ('Dona nobis pacem') but re-flected more modern tastes with arias both tuneful ('Et in Spiritum sanctum') and *affektvoll* ('Benedictus'). Neither builder nor composer, in their respective skills, was able or willing quite to suspend his trad-itional working methods, follow mere fashion or betray the meticulous care he had always taken, whatever his critics said. There is nothing facilely *galant* about the solo 'Benedictus', and Scheibe would still have found its beauty more obscure than that of a Handel aria of the same period.

It is doubtful if anyone noticed the various symmetries in the com-pleted mass: the arrangement of choruses and arias in the Credo, or the massive plan of the whole whereby the middle movement has the most original scoring ('Quoniam'). Whatever the circumstances in Dresden, there were also personal reasons for making such a compendium of styles and structures, in particular the pious duty Bach gave himself of developing music beyond easy solutions. There may have been practical reasons for reusing an already reused movement for the final chorus, quite as much as there was when Handel pilfered his own and other composers' works, but in the mass there is no sense of slack endeavour. For such a believer as Bach, the three texts associated with its final movement – 'We thank you, O Lord' (in German and in Latin) and 'Give us peace' – were entirely compatible, whatever practical reasons there were for reusing material.

Similarly, music celebrating the blessings of the kingdom of Saxony in Cantata 215 could also serve the 'Osanna' in the royal mass. Or the kind of love duet familiar in the king's operas could be elevated into the exquisite scoring and *affektvoll* beauty of the 'Domine Deus' aria. Earlier parody, as in the St Mark Passion of 1731 which used movements from Cantatas 198, 54, 7 and perhaps others, had evidently been much simpler and less systematic. In the mass's reusing and revising of so much older material – at least twenty of its twenty-four movements are reworked compositions – the composer was carefully and systematically searching for a compendium of types and styles of music, ancient and modern, delicate and massive. As with a great piece of architecture, interesting (and vital to professionals) though its technical and structural details are, the true wonder of the mass is its world of sound, unique, rich, totally assured, calming or stimulating as the case may be. Its five- and eight-part choruses alone immediately transport the listener to this sound-world, one entirely different from that of the Passions. To hear in it now the final, generous offering of a creative lifetime's experience in music of so many kinds is more than mere hindsight.

Broadly considered, the quarrels with Scheibe and Ernesti (see below) could well reflect in their different ways a general lowering of expectation for church music and of its position in even such a city as Leipzig. That there were apparently no complaints against Bach in his last decade at St Thomas's could mean simply that he and the authorities had settled to a *modus vivendi* of lower expectations generally, that he was free to use music from elsewhere and so to escape into his own interests. These he certainly had: the intense study of canon, fugue and counterpoint, further work on organ music associated with Advent and Christmas (the Seven Fughettas, the Canonic Variations, the Schübler and other chorales), and the final grandiose compendium for the Roman mass. Scheibe probably knew little of Bach's recent music, either that which pointed in the new directions taken by secular music (concertos, sonatas, burlescas) or that which was soon to govern higher music study (counterpoint, fugue, four-part harmonisation). He would surely have had no idea that the second of these would continue to bring Bach to the fore for countless students over the next two centuries.

The reduced significance of sacred music generally in Protestant countries affected by the cultural changes now variously labelled Rationalism, Secularism or the Enlightenment left music to blossom in other realms, some only just then emerging. Bach's intense work in counterpoint was reflecting current views of music as a science, and would certainly be so treated by the younger generation, especially after his death. Irrespective of its pedagogical potential, however, such intense work was in itself the typical sign of a mature composer's tendency towards the abstract, the transcendental and the economy of means by which the merely entertaining is stripped away.

> He knew how to give harpsichords so pure and correct a temperament in their tuning that all keys sounded beautiful and pleasing.

It can only be guessed how long-standing a desire of Bach this had been, or whether the authors, as Bach pupils, were dominated by thoughts of what was to be the great new manual for teachers of counterpoint, composition and keyboard playing, namely the two books of the *Well-Tempered Clavier*.

Though now frequently referred to in temperament and performance-practice studies, the Obituary's remark matches a little too closely later eighteenth-century tastes to be taken at face value. After all, roughly contemporary with the original Book I had been sets of Inventions that still did not use all twenty-four keys, only fifteen.

Despite their own limited harmonic imagination as composers, musicians of 1750 wanted to be able to play in any key at any time, especially perhaps on the new pianos, whose tone production, being less immediate than that of the harpsichord and less sustained than that of the organ, made equal temperament less and less objectionable. G. A. Sorge's report that Bach did not like the 'four bad triads' of earlier temperaments similarly dates from 1748:[13] it says nothing about his earlier practice. Besides, Sorge was something of a tuning crank and liked involving Bach in his theories, as tuning cranks still do.

In speaking here of 'Clavicymbale', 'harpsichords', the authors seem to be visualising the composer tuning his various instruments in daily use. Not only were organs more the concern of professional builders, and much less often tuned, but they remained closer to older tunings, and their music required far fewer than twenty-four keys. It was a sign of the modern aspirations of *Clavierübung* III that it began and ended in E flat major, a 'beautiful, majestic key' not in the 'head and fingers' of most organists, at least in Hamburg (according to Mattheson 1731, p. 244). This collection also contained chorales in F sharp minor and F minor, but they did not require organ (they have no pedal part) and suit the harpsichord well – hence, indeed, these keys? On the other hand, at least a stop or two of the organ in St Thomas's, Leipzig, such as a Stopped Diapason in the chair organ, could have been tuned close to equal temperament for the remote keys it needed in cantatas. When, to make up for its high pitch, it had to accompany in D flat a cantata movement composed in E flat, a single stop or two could have been appropriately tuned: a stop at lower pitch was often included in larger organs, and to include one instead in equal or near-equal temperament was feasible.

The markedly unequal temperament of most organs was not necessarily a disadvantage. On the contrary, it gave 'piquancy' to an early chorale in F minor in the *Orgelbüchlein* (the thinnest texture in the book), and a 'sense of excitement' to remote modulations in the big D major

---

[13] Major triads on F sharp, A flat, B major and C sharp: see *Dok* II, p. 450.

fugue. Nor should it be forgotten that old associations of key left even a work such as the *Art of Fugue* with an important allusion: its D minor recalls the old 'first key' (*tonus primus, le premier ton*) and should have a relaxed character, one quite distinct from the keys either side, C minor ('pathetic') and E minor ('elegiac'). When a tuning leaves keys with particular characteristics, Bach's modal sensitivities become more striking, as in his two kinds of G major. The modern key of G, diatonic and with strong dominants, is clear in harpsichord toccatas or suites; the older key of G, mixolydian and tending towards the subdominant, is clear in many an organ chorale. Mature organ works still observed this distinction, as in the chorales for the Trinity BWV 676 (diatonic) and Ten Commandments BWV 678 (modal). In vocal music, the accompanying instruments will still observe sufficient differences between keys as to impart a particular character to each, and it is clear that the *St Matthew Passion* does not survey its array of keys only to have them sound all the same only a little higher or lower from movement to movement.

A special problem concerns the *Well-Tempered Clavier*, in particular Book I. Although 'well-tempered' was not identical to 'equal-tempered' in German use and usage, it could well be synonymous in the context of a set of pieces in all the keys, and there is still a general assumption not only that equal temperament was intended but that Bach wrote the WTC to vindicate or demonstrate it. Yet even if it were 100 per cent possible, equal temperament is not necessary for WTC I. And to discard the option of retuning between movements is itself to make assumptions – for example, that WTC is a cycle to be played as such according to modern concert conventions. Besides, there is some difficulty in believing that in itself temperament was of vital importance to so creative a master of harmony as J. S. Bach. Is he not likely to have been much more interested in the definitive difference between major and minor keys?

The title page of Book I (the second set, now called Book II, has no title) says nothing about temperaments but carefully specifies that all the keys are here, 'both with respect to the major third or C–D–E and as concerns the minor third or D–E–F' ('so wohl *tertiam majorem* oder *Ut Re Mi* anlangend, als auch *tertiam minorem* oder *Re Mi Fa* betreffend'). So what is important is that all the majors and all the minors are to be found in the book, not that all semitones are equal. One has only to think of the totally different effect and *Affekt* of the opening two preludes – a C major arpeggio with two Es, bright, gentle, then a C minor chord, darker, sombre, agitated – to suppose that it was the promise of such contrasts that was so important, not whether C sharp major was tuned exactly like C major only a semitone higher. A similar and contemporary interest in the differences between major and minor can be sensed in those sonatas of Domenico Scarlatti in which an anxious passage in the minor suddenly opens into the sunlight of the major (e.g. Sonata in A minor Kk 175).

Note that the Obituary authors neither mention equal temperament nor, with their words 'pure and correct' ('rein und richtig'), do they imply any particularly expert grasp of the niceties of tuning, since in post-Renaissance music a 'correct' interval would not be 'pure'. ('Rein' was also the word used by Emanuel for his father's violin playing. But presumably his violin fifths were more *rein* than his harpsichord fifths.) Elsewhere, Emanuel said that his father did his own harpsichord quilling as well as tuning, and did not thank others for doing it (*Dok* III, p. 285. Was 'others' Emanuel himself?). All of these remarks aim to fill out the picture of a composer knowledgable and assiduous in practical matters, as no doubt he was. But it is a picture drawn by a younger generation of composers of whom, I imagine, few could re-leather a piano hammer or would expect to be called upon to do so.

> Of his moral character those might speak who have enjoyed dealings and friendship with him and have witnessed his honesty towards God and his neighbour.

The Lutheran duty towards 'God and one's neighbour' will be discussed later in the chapter. Bach's annotations in the Calov Bible to the Book of Leviticus, the law book of the Old Testament, suggest him to have had a particular interest in rules and regulations. At the same time, even his few letters as they exist hint in various ways at a fond *paterfamilias* and a man with long-lasting friendships. References to his two grandsons and to the marriage of his daughter (Dok I, pp. 118–19) are matched by the personal contacts from Weissenfels and Cöthen being kept up in Leipzig (Dok II, pp. 394, 181). Standing godfather to his daughter's first-born (Dok II, p. 459) is only one instance of such traditional ties. The romantic picture of a hard-working but urbane family man who enjoyed boisterous gatherings, with music, tomfoolery and food, might not be far from the truth.

If Bach's un-docile responses to criticism and to the machinations of those around him appear aggressive, truculent or at least self-protective, a positive interpretation would be that all the abuse he perceived – however irascible or simply impatient he was by nature – got in the way of his composition, his creative duty as he saw it. (One might discern something comparable in Wagner's autobiography, *Mein Leben*.) Straightforward ambition, as when he left Mühlhausen for Weimar after only a year, to the chagrin of the council (Dok II, p. 405) and before he had seen the organ project through, was not unreasonable. To counter the usual adulation of J. S. Bach by accusations of an 'unmistakable harsh edge . . . famously confrontational . . . a pervasive sense of persecution and an attitude of spiteful defiance' (Marshall 2000, p. 502) would be an exaggeration in the other direction. Rather, he could simply have found that, unlike the Weimar duke or the Cöthen prince, the church and school superiors in Leipzig stood in the way of his work as a musician, hence the Obituary authors describing (hearing him say?) how well his art had been appreciated in different ways in his two previous appointments.

Here are six particular moments of contention from his Leipzig years, some more serious than others:

September 1723: Bach made a claim on the university for the right he had, as Thomascantor, to direct music in a certain number of services, for a fee. On being allowed only half the fee, he appealed to the elector (king) in Dresden and had a ruling in his favour.

Good Friday 1724: Seeming (disingenuously?) to be unaware that it was the turn of St Nicholas's church to have the great Passion performance (St John) this year, Bach had a notice printed advertising St Thomas's. On being compelled to readvertise, he insisted that the gallery and harpsichord of St Nicholas be improved. The following year, he revived the work for St Thomas's.

October 1727: A paid commission to supply and perform the Funeral Ode to a text written by the university professor of poetry J. C. Gottsched (Cantata 198) for the later Electress Christiane Eberhardine went ahead against the objections of the then university organist. (The composer directed the performance from the harpsichord.)

September 1728: St Thomas's subdeacon insisted on choosing hymns for vespers, a traditional right of cantors, who saw vespers as giving an opportunity for music of more than usual interest. A ruling in favour of the subdeacon.

August 1730: Bach was reproached by the Thomas School council for dismissing a chorister, being absent without leave, failing to teach (i.e. in some or all of the seven hours' musical instruction scheduled per week) or supervise his substitute (and without offering an explanation), failing to take a singing class, showing little pleasure in work, and generally being 'incorrigibel' (*Dok* II, pp. 205–6). In November 1734, he was criticised again for not teaching.

August 1736: A long, bitter quarrel with the new rector (headmaster), J. A. Ernesti, over who had the right to appoint the choir prefect. Documents show Bach appealing in turn to the rector, the council, the consistory and the king, none with clear success; they also suggest that since his authority was questioned in this way, he had found difficulty with discipline in the school and the choir. The king may have ruled in his favour: he named him court composer three months later and was greeted with a cantata on a visit to Leipzig after Easter 1738 (the lost BWV Anh. I 13).

Note that although these arguments were largely about territory, and affecting both the status and the income of the cantor, none of them was about avoiding work as a composer: on the contrary. In the case of Cantata 198, some exceptionally beautiful music resulted, being a work for an especially grand event in which, for once, he and all the authorities of town, university and church participated. As for choosing hymns, organists today trying to maintain artistic standards against obstreperous or trendy clergy can guess what was involved, given Bach's obvious devotion all his life to Luther's texts and the hymn repertory of the pristine Reformation. The very orthodoxy of the texts of chorales used for *Clavierübung* III and so many cantatas begins to look like a gesture, for Bach doubtless knew that St Thomas's was originally a church of the Augustinian Order to which Luther had belonged.

As for the school board's complaint, Bach had had collegial enough relations with the former headmaster in 1733 to join him in an appeal about a parishioner obliged to pay them fees for his recent marriage outside Leipzig (Dok I, pp. 75–6). Ernesti was twenty-two years younger than Bach, so the question is whether, in 1736, it was the case of a young man standing on his dignity and authority or of an older being resistant and unwilling to change an established habit. Both, perhaps. Bach had already been criticised for lapses in school teaching during the process to appoint Ernesti in 1734, and the new rector was soon complaining that Bach did not rehearse the boys enough (Dok II, pp. 252, 265).

The Ernesti situation was especially bad, dragging on for months and still being reported on forty years later (Dok III, p. 314). Both contestants made clear that there was a total breakdown of personal relations, especially the rector, who devoted a great deal of time, energy and rhetorical literacy to put his case that:

Bach fails to defer to the rector over prefects, as regulations say he must.
He twice caused commotion in church by chasing away the unwanted prefect.
He is insubordinate.
He thinks it beneath his dignity to direct wedding music if this consists only of hymns.

Bach answers the various points more succinctly and straightforwardly. This alone may be responsible for the rector's further irritation, for once more he indulged at length in elegant, quasi-objective prose to complain that:

Bach's account is neither complete nor truthful ('wahrhaftig': Dok II, pp. 274ff.).

He had intended and wished ('intention gehabt und gewünschet') the replacement prefect to make a mistake.

So Bach is stubborn, insubordinate, devious, untruthful, vindictive and malicious. His defence is to ask the consistory court for protection so that he can get on with his duties.

Whether in the autumn of 1736 he was drawn to Dresden for royal support in the quarrel, or for a superior job at court itself, or because he admired Dresden's musical potential, is not clear. Nor is the degree to which Ernesti's complaints were prompted by his petty resentment at a subordinate having friends in high places. But the situation is not hard to imagine: school, church and town authorities could not act as despotically as a prince but could take other steps to make life hard for an insufficiently humble composer who wanted to be left alone to create music. One response would be for him to tend to neglect other duties, and there are hints of this ever after the Ernesti quarrel, and indeed earlier. Today, a Master of Cathedral Music, sooner or later vexed by clergy, might well react by becoming even more devoted to his art and focusing on its higher calling. At the same time, one can easily believe that the fault is not all on one side.

It must have been further aggravation for Bach, therefore, that during the late 1730s he was also criticised as a creative composer (the Scheibe review, above) and met with objections against his perhaps proudest creations, the big Passion performances. His clear irritation at the latter could alone account for any declining productivity in his last decade as cantor, just as temporarily giving up the Collegium concerts in the spring or summer of 1737 may be some kind of response to the Ernesti quarrel. Depression, tension, strain? Working on the Goldberg Variations around 1740, and through them concentrating his thoughts on writing for the harpsichord, on canonic counterpoint and on virtuoso solo music making – none of which related to St Thomas's and its activities – does look like a deliberate turn in other directions.

Although Bach was on record as admiring the music of Handel and C. H. Graun, his occasional use of their music over these years could be seen as another form of shrugging off obligations and 'giving people what they want'. In saying so little about Leipzig, the Obituary does give the impression of a falling-off in the composer's commitment to the job. Nevertheless, both Passions were probably performed again in his final years, and one easily imagines his creative energy *ad gloriam Dei* to have been irrepressible, despite the many vexations with which he was incapable of dealing supinely. Hence the late works, both the 'abstract' and the 'practical'.

How sociable Bach was outside his family, even how warm his professional contacts were, cannot be established from hard evidence. Especially when compared with Mainwaring's biography of Handel, it is striking how little the Obituary ever refers to other musicians or other people. While this produces the desired picture of a self-dependent composer – think how much more detail Emanuel could have given of his father's musical activities and contacts! – its virtual silence may have another reason: he had latterly become a lone master. Special musical challenges, such as making sure that the intricate counterpoint of the *Art of Fugue* remained playable on the keyboard, must have taken even Johann Sebastian Bach huge amounts of time, with meticulous work, bar by bar, piece by piece. The seclusion necessary for this was not only physical but spiritual, for this musical world had not been penetrated before, unlike Handel's more or less static fund of regurgitated musical ideas. The recherché nature of much of what Bach wrote is easy to imagine as the work of a recluse, actual or, at the very least, potential.

> Indeed, our late Bach did not involve himself in deep, theoretical speculations [*Betrachtungen*] about music but was all the stronger in the doing of it.

Though Emanuel said later that this particular Obituary remark was owed to Lorenz Mizler and 'is not worth much', he too observed that

Bach was 'no lover of dry, mathematical paraphernalia' (Dok III, p. 288). This rather goes with Bach's supplying no biography when asked, or publishing big volumes of music with no preface, unlike others of the time such as Kauffmann in *Harmonische Seelenlust* (1733) and Maichelbeck in his *VIII Sonaten* (1736). Was this reticence a form of modesty or its opposite?

In 1738, Mizler, a former pupil, founded a Corresponding Society of Musical Sciences, a scattered group of musicians exchanging letters on matters of theory or 'musical science' which Bach eventually joined as fourteenth member in 1747. The 'deep, theoretical speculations' of which Mizler spoke would have concerned music as 'part of philosophical learning', the subject of his original master's dissertation in Leipzig in 1734, dedicated predictably to Mattheson. Mizler's notion of 'philosophy' and his preoccupation with the 'mathematical grounds for composition', however, aroused even Mattheson's scepticism (Dok II, p. 380), and it is highly unlikely that other invited members of his society, such as Telemann, Handel and C. H. Graun, spent any more time on such things than Bach did.

When Handel was named honorary member in 1745, Mizler had already mentioned in print Handel's refusal of an honorary Oxford doctorate (HHB, pp. 396, 376). Can this have been an incentive for Bach to join the Corresponding Society when Mizler approached him in 1747? Or perhaps he had previously delayed because of having a quite different idea of 'deep, theoretical speculation'. Obviously, deep thought is necessary for the fugues, canons, motivic complexities and various kinds of intimate musical allusion in Bach's music, throughout his life and especially in the last decade. But he could well have openly shunned textbook calculations of interval ratios and the like, hence Emanuel's criticism of Mizler's remark. After all, the *Art of Fugue* was a 'doing of' music, not a 'theoretical speculation'.

Claiming to be unlearned before a certain kind of pedant is something that occurs elsewhere in music, as when G. B. Doni remarked in 1638 that Frescobaldi did not know a major from a minor semitone (Gallico 1986, pp. 187–8) or that Monteverdi showed 'little understanding' when he, Doni, tried to arouse his interest in micro-tunings (Palisca 1994, p. 487). For Monteverdi, Frescobaldi and J. S. Bach all to be judged guilty, there must be something wrong with the judges. Mizler could well have been one of those gifted people, still to be met with, who never quite marshal their mastery of several disciplines – music theory, theology, philosophy, medicine, law, rhetoric, physics, mathematics, publishing – into a genuine, mainline musicianship.

Perhaps it was Handel's membership that prompted Bach to con-tribute to Mizler's society pieces of a distinct 'scientific' character, as a part of the annual offering each member was supposed to make: hence the Canonic Variations for organ (1747) and also the six-part canon BWV 1076 (one of the canons added by the composer to his copy of the Goldbergs). Perhaps some of the canons of the Art of Fugue were pieces he would also have submitted, according to the society's practice, had he remained a member for longer. Another corresponding society of sorts had been Mattheson's Critica musica of two or three decades earlier, to which musicians including Bach's predecessor Kuhnau had contributed, writing on musical-historical topics rather than theoret-ical. Presumably Bach knew that Kuhnau had done this, and always gave Mattheson a wide berth. And perhaps like Emanuel he also found Fux's Gradus ad Parnassum 'a dry kind of counterpoint' (Dok III, p. 289) and said so – hence Mizler did not dedicate his translation of it to Bach when he published it in Leipzig in 1742? This is something that might otherwise have been expected, considering Bach's position as director musices lipsiensis and his recent interest, some of it published, in the very counterpoint covered by the book.

The many instances of the numbers 14 (Bach), 41 (J. S. Bach) and 158 (Johann Sebastian Bach) that can be found in the music – if one counts the number of bars in a section or piece, or its number of notes, or even its number of movements – fit in with the use of simple ciphers as found in the writings of Werckmeister, Kuhnau and others. How many instances are likely to be conscious, where and for what reason, are all open questions and just now and then important. For in-stance, if the Fourteen Canons attached to the Goldberg Variations are a self-reference (14 = Bach), might this be merely something appropriate to an arcane genre (monothematic canons) and so not transferable to another? One can discover other number references, such as ten entries for the melody of the Ten Commandments chorale in Cantata 77 or the many threes (perceptual and conceptual) in *Clavierübung* III; and there are also perceptible references to the notes B A C H (B♭ A C B♮) in far more places than the late Canonic Variations and *Art of Fugue*. Supposed divine proportions in cantata movements (i.e. a proportional structure in which a natural division or conspicuous moment occurs about two-thirds of the way through) are matched by supposed gematria (i.e. note names having number equivalents and producing patterns) in the works for solo violin and who knows what else.

But any enthusiasm now to seek out such things needs to be tempered by several considerations. First, the desire to prove that they are not imaginary will lead inevitably to further conjecture, such as that they serve some deep symbolic purpose. There is no verifiable limit to such conjecture, only common sense. Secondly, hypotheses ought also to account for both the negative (why are Golden Sections not discernible in other music?) and the comparative (what other music can be interpreted in the same way? what other numbers are operating?). Thirdly, most numbers involve simple musical events and are only reminders in the music of words or ideas outside it, a kind of 'pay attention!' – they are not subtle tokens of some confessional hermeticism or personal psychology. Rather than a sign of 'deep, theoretical speculation', they are the work of a composer 'all the stronger in the doing of' music itself, as the Obituary said.

> In the multiplicity of his song [*mannigfaltigem Gesang*], he delighted, taught and moved young people, women, men, princes, kings and all real connoisseurs.

These words, from a poetic cantata text supplied at the end of the Obituary by Georg Venzky, another member of Mizler's society, give its only reference to Bach's teaching, except for the reference to 'not a few fine organists' at Weimar. The poem probably meant 'taught' in a broader sense: his music was instructive as well as delightful and moving, both teaching and stirring those who listened especially to his settings of Scripture. It is also clear from Bach's many extant testimonials for students that he supported their studies warmly, and helped as conscientiously in their job applications as many a teacher does today. Though no doubt his sons and son-in-law-to-be received most attention in this respect, he may well have spoken or written on behalf of students on even more occasions than is now recorded.

When after 1750 the position of J. S. Bach the Universal Instructor developed, when pupils spread what they understood of his gospel in their various appointments in central Germany, so more was said about his methods as a teacher. In 1782 J. P. Kirnberger, in writing his own book, claimed to follow his teacher's method in composition by going by step from the easiest to the most difficult, so that fugue writing can be taken in one's stride (*Dok* III, p. 362). H. N. Gerber was said much later by his son to have studied the playing of inventions, suites and then fugues, going on eventually to figured-bass work based on good part writing ('in the singing of the voices together': *Dok* III, p. 476). These and other references are close to Emanuel's replies in 1775 to queries from Forkel who, in helping to create a German tradition for musical instruction, wanted to know who influenced Bach and how or what he taught his pupils. According to Emanuel, learning four-part harmony was the first task, including harmonising chorales and realising figured bass. If a boy, including Bach's own sons, did not evince the gift of invention ('Erfindung'), he was not taken on as a student in composition (*Dok* III, p. 289). How untypical of musical instruction in general any of this was, however, is unclear, although Bach undoubtedly had a much more active life as a teacher than the Handels and Vivaldis of the period.

Despite the various references to teaching, there is little evidence that any pupil, Bach sons or otherwise, understood the power that one might now see as typical of him above all others: his sense of harmonic drive. Like many pupils, Johann Ludwig Krebs, in Leipzig from 1726 to 1737, could imitate techniques or approaches or particular themes, as in his settings of 'Ach Herr' (compare the opening of Bach's Cantata 135) or 'Christ lag' (compare the *Orgelbüchlein* chorale BWV 624), and he was an intelligent, musical learner. But his music has no such tension. Although J. A. Scheibe may well have studied concerto form with Bach (see Wollny 2002a, pp. 138–9), and goes promisingly through the motions of theme and binary form in a solo concerto, he fails in a similar way, as does H. N. Gerber in his imitations of the two-part Inventions. In the case of Emanuel Bach, a sonata's or concerto's fine opening gesture, some shifting tonalities, chromatic effects and an agitated bass line of repeated notes are all unlikely to disguise the paucity of real harmonic drive, as well as an absence of the intricate and logical form he could have observed in his father's movements. 'He promised much' might be the epitaph of many a Bach pupil, alas.

No doubt some of this failure results from different tastes or criteria, as for example when Krebs's Praeludium in F minor makes use of Bach's Praeludium in B minor BWV 544 and dilutes its intensity, as if responding to a modern taste for pleasant, less demanding music. Was Krebs resisting his teacher's harmonic grasp or was he incapable of building on it? Or did Bach simply not teach it, leaving it to be realised only in his own works? Lessons, judging from Gerber's notebook, were taken up more with the grammar of imitative and invertible counterpoint, and with shaping simple movements including the new *galant* dances. The Allemande in the *Clavierbüchlein* for W. F. Bach already mentioned (see above, pp. 86–7) suggests at least that Bach taught pupils how to construct a binary movement with good phraseology and competent modulations. On the whole, however, none of them, not even Friedemann Bach, could do much more than turn in quite other directions, leaving the B minor Mass and *Art of Fugue* protruding like unscalable peaks from the effete novelties of the 1740s and 1750s.

It can only be guessed how Bach taught his early pupils, before the time when he had at hand the Inventions, French Suites, *Well-Tempered Clavier* I and eventually, for figured-bass work, the books of J. D. Heinichen (1711) and F. E. Niedt (1721). His own study as a child was probably conventional – regular or irregular instruction from family members in the profession, musical odd jobs, occasional participation in making music or preparing works, and personal observation as keen as ability and self-motivation allowed. In the sense that he 'studied' with Buxtehude, so pupils continued to come to him, from his twenties onwards. Perhaps it was in part Bach's systematic method of private musical instruction in Leipzig that led Emanuel to draw the picture of him as a more informally, self-taught musician himself. Except from anecdotes, Emanuel would have known little of how the Buxtehudes, Böhms and Bachs of the day had learnt music.

Judging by Bach's early chorale harmonisations, in which the organist ran his fingers over scales and flourishes between the lines of the hymn, it was from handling chorales in church that a musician might learn both the arts of service playing and the first steps in composition. The two rather went together, and this would be so especially at a period when most hymnbooks did not contain even melodies, much less harmonisations. Other chorale settings suggest that players were taught to master particular techniques, such as variation or canon or double pedal parts, all represented in various 'spurious works of Bach' composed either by his pupils or young musicians elsewhere. Musical youth wishing to learn the arts of composing concertos, chamber music and above all opera would not be studying with J. S. Bach either in Weimar or in Leipzig but would be off to Hamburg or Venice.

> His sight, rather poor by nature, and weakened yet further by his unheard-of enthusiasm for study . . . brought him, in his last years, in the way of an eye disease. Partly from the desire to serve God and his neighbour further . . . he wanted to improve this by an operation.

The Lutheran formula 'for God and his neighbour' is already found in the couplet on the title page of the *Orgelbüchlein*, appropriate both for an organist's hymnbook and for his duty to the community as a musician. The formula crops up often. In a testimonial of 1743, Bach had praised a student for his endeavours to be of service to 'God and the *res publica*', or community (*Dok* I, p. 146). At much the same time, G. A. Sorge, in a dedication of some sonatas to Bach, praised him for 'love of his neighbour', adding that this was something 'commanded on high' but rarely found amongst 'conceited and self-loving virtuosi' (*Dok* II, p. 413). Pairing 'God and one's neighbour' recalls the pairing 'connoisseur and amateur' met with at the time, for both have pious allusion. When a work such as the Goldberg Variations was prepared for 'the delight of the souls of music lovers', 'delight' ('Ergötzung') says more than it seems to say, implying recreation in a spiritual sense, preparation before continuing God's work.

Evidently, either Emanuel or his father felt obliged to give a reason for the surgery to cure his cataracts, a condition probably brought on by untreated diabetes. 'Rather poor by nature' might refer to a gradual deterioration of his eyesight over the last twenty years. In any case, he wanted to be of further service as a composer, and eyesight problems were yet another vexation, another hindrance to that work. But the surgery was dangerous, as events proved, and in the end everyone, neighbour, widow, children, his Maker, was deprived by the sad outcome. The modesty suggested in the Obituary's remark matches not only the brevity of Bach's entry in Walther's *Lexicon* but his total absence from J. H. Zedler's compendious *Universal-Lexicon* of 1731, another book published in Leipzig. All this does suggest him to have been an exception to the 'conceited and self-loving virtuosi' of the day, anxious for his rights in other respects though he seems to have been.

It was probably just before the Easter Fair of 1750 that Bach was operated on twice for cataracts, by the visiting English eye surgeon John Taylor, whose treatment eight years later of the blind Handel was also less than successful (*HHB*, p. 520). In the month following surgery Bach took in his last residential student, J. G. Müthel, presumably hoping to remain active, though the last music he wrote down himself was probably parts of the B minor Mass and J. C. Bach's motet 'Lieber Herr Gott, wecke uns auf', in late 1749 or early 1750. Whether like Handel he then used amanuenses, as distinct from copyists, is not known for certain, although the anecdote of a chorale 'dictated in his blindness' (see below) implies the arrangements he had to make over his last half-year. No doubt various pupils and children (including Elisabeth, married to J. C. Altnickol on 20 January 1749) could on occasion have served in this way.

He certainly kept up instruction for pupils, and according to his last signed letter of 11 December 1749, had had one of them, J. N. Bammler, direct the entire church music for him 'in his absence' (BJ 1997, p. 41). This last phrase is likely to denote indisposition rather than professional absence. Extant MSS show that for some months from autumn 1748 on, his handwriting and presumably eyesight had deteriorated. For him to appoint a deputy was important in view of an event of 8 June 1749, when representatives of the town council auditioned Gottlob Harrer as the next cantor – a 'future replacement, should the decease of Mr Bach come about at some point', in the words of the minister president of Saxony (Dok II, p. 456).

Evidently the minister president had visited Leipzig previously, and either found Bach already unwell or was taking precautions to have his own capellmeister primed for this key position, one potentially close to the interests of the Dresden court. The audition certainly suggests that Bach's health was deteriorating, but how tactless, precipitous or merely sensible the town council's audition was is not clear. It was certainly not against tradition, for Bach's predecessor had been treated similarly many years before; moreover, since only a day after his eventual death six applicants for the job were being discussed, they must have applied beforehand, in anticipation. That Harrer's audition took place not in church but in the concert room of the Three Swans could be seen as either underhand or discreet – or simply as deferring to Bach's authority in the town's churches, as per contract.

Although the known order of events during the late period is sketchy, work seems to have continued on details of the Art of Fugue, preparatory to its actual engraving then under way, and even more intensively on the newer movements of the B minor Mass. It is not difficult to imagine the motives prompting an aging composer to enlarge the massive compilations of musical technique represented by these two unique works, one instrumental the other choral, one containing new creations the other radical revisions. Such time-consuming works of large dimensions, neither of which was part of a cantor's duties, need not mean a turning-away from the Thomaskirche and its music, however, since Bach had long had his own reasons for making collections of music and was, it seems, seldom deterred. Deteriorating sight would explain the declining quality of his manuscript, but there had been at least some big musical performances in his penultimate year: St John Passion on Good Friday 1749 and the Easter Oratorio two days later.

> On 28 July 1750, after a quarter past eight in the evening, in the sixty-sixth year of his life, he passed away gently and peacefully through the merit of his Redeemer.

In claiming that the surgery and subsequent treatment overthrew his whole system, which succumbed eventually to a final stroke and fever, the Obituary authors speak as if they were eye-witnesses to Bach's last six months. But there is no evidence of this, and the final period of discomfort was probably nearer three than six months. Although the Obituary twice speaks of his powers of body and mind as otherwise undiminished, various symptoms and characteristics in the late handwriting have more recently been interpreted as indicating advanced diabetes (BJ 1990, pp. 53–64), chronic rather than acute, exacerbated by age, and no doubt worsened by the surgery and its subsequent infections (Dok II, p. 470). Bach took communion at home on 22 July, and on the day of his death presumably Anna Magdalena and the younger children were present.

The story of the blind composer dictating the chorale 'Wenn wir in höchsten Nöten sein' ('When we are in highest need') is a puzzle, especially for the modern reader who wants neither to dismiss any such heart-warming anecdote nor to be misled by it if it is unreliable. The story was told in a note prefacing the Art of Fugue, whose publication was probably initiated by the main legatees (Anna Magdalena, Friedemann, Emanuel, son-in-law Altnickol), one of whom (Anna Magdalena? Altnickol?) could have relayed the story. It does not say that the piece was dictated 'on his deathbed' but 'in his blindness', and this may have had no greater significance than Handel's use of an amanuensis when his sight failed. Virtually the same chorale was copied by someone (daughter Elisabeth?) into a late MS collection of chorales and given there the title 'Before your throne I stand', which does indeed seem appropriate to a deathbed. But when it was copied, who gave it this title and on whose authority it was copied is not known: it might be there in the chorale album with no more authority than, under its other title, it is in the Art of Fugue.

Furthermore, since the setting was in part over thirty years old (a version of an *Orgelbüchlein* chorale), it can hardly have been dictated entirely from scratch. Nor is the counterpoint much more than humdrum. In that case, if the anecdote is really true, what the composer's priorities were in his decline become clear: the music, void of notable invention and special or inimitable hallmarks, in no way 'interferes' with the text, which is a prayer. Simple means heartfelt. On the other hand, if the anecdote is untrue or mistaken, then there need be no certainty even that J. S. Bach composed it: any competent student familiar both with the *Orgelbüchlein* chorale and the smaller Confessional chorale published in *Clavierübung* III (BWV 687) could have cobbled it together. Hence the puzzle.

Frequently, death notices and other reports gave the time of death, which in this case was recorded as 'about eight o'clock' (Dok II, pp. 472, 473). When Handel died, a newspaper reported death at 'a little before eight o'clock' on Easter Saturday 14 April 1759, but his doctor claimed that it was the night before, Good Friday, a more significant day (HHB, p. 529). On 6 August 1750, a Berlin newspaper reported Bach's death, adding that the loss of this uncommonly gifted man would be much regretted by all true connoisseurs of music. That may be so, but in Leipzig the poet Gottsched, voluble on other occasions, apparently wrote nothing.

On 30 or 31 July, Bach was buried in the Johanniskirche churchyard, east of the city walls and through the Grimma Gate, a church whose organ he had participated in examining in 1744 (see above, p. 165). The Obituary does not mention the church by name, or show any sign of this being a possible matter of interest to its readers. From neither Obituary nor any other source is anything known of a funeral or committal service or of what music was sung, though colleagues and the choir were present as the body was taken to the cemetery church, presumably in a procession and presumably singing chorales (*Dok* II, p. 474). It is possible that J. C. Bach's motet already mentioned had been copied out by him and his student-assistant Bammler for that very occasion: 'Lord God, wake us up' is an apt funerary text, and the motet's composer was to receive special praise in the Obituary. By contrast, Handel some time before his death had requested permission to be buried in Westminster Abbey, and left money for a monument, though he too desired his eventual burial to be 'in a private manner' (*HHB*, p. 528).

A coffin of oak supposed to be Bach's was opened in 1894, placed in the rebuilt Johanniskirche in 1900, moved to the Thomaskirche in 1949, and, in the course of further work in the church in 1962–4, reinterred in its present position near the crossing. There can be no absolute certainty that the remains are his, for though the well-known bust made from a skull impression accords with the authentic Haussmann portraits of 1746 and 1748, the latter were known to the sculptor and somewhat idealised.

Handel left £17,500 in annuities plus £48 in chattels (*HHB*, pp. 533, 539), at a time when a new two-manual harpsichord cost about £70; Bach left some 1,122 thaler in chattels, books and instruments, including a two-manual harpsichord worth 80 (*Dok* II, p. 496). By the time of his death, Handel had amassed over eighty paintings, including some 'very good ones' (*HHB*, p. 534). There is no comparison, therefore, between their financial positions, though in both cases the composers' manuscripts and musical scores were not counted in the estate but bequeathed separately and previously. This was done by Handel formally

12 Bust of J. S. Bach.
Made by Karl Seffner in 1895, based on a hypothetical reconstruction of the feaures of
a skull exhumed in the churchyard of the Johanniskirche in 1894 and claimed to be
that of the composer in Wilhelm His, *Johann Sebastian Bach: Forschungen über dessen
Grabstätte*, Leipzig, 1895.

('my Music Books' to J. C. Smith: HHB, p. 441), by Bach only reputedly
(chiefly between the widow and two eldest sons). Smith was a careful curator, passing the autographs on to his son, who gave them to
the king's library which lodged them in the British Museum. Philipp

Emanuel accumulated and preserved his father's MSS reasonably well but not Wilhelm Friedemann, whose materials are mostly lost, despite the reverence in which his father was held in the later eighteenth century. That reverence, expressed so often with respect to Bach's contrapuntal skill, seems to have been directed less warmly to the vocal works, chamber sonatas and instrumental concertos, which in common perception were superseded by the Italianate operas, symphonies, quartets and concertos of the next generation of composers.

APPENDIX 1: A SAMPLE HYPOTHESIS

The sparseness of evidence about the daily activities, feelings and thoughts of J. S. Bach has meant that later biographies, increasingly preoccupied with the personal and private, have resorted to speculation in these areas. Writers have glimpsed in documents the beginning of answers to such questions as 'What kind of person, husband, father, teacher, colleague was he?' or 'What did he like or dislike?', but for many reasons the glimpse might be quite misleading. Much of the present book already questions what the evidence appears to say.

Nevertheless, some questions are less nebulous, particularly in relation to professional matters such as 'What did he regard his responsibilities/privileges to be?', even if the most revealing episodes known about are his quarrels. When he made particular journeys, presumably at some trouble, ambition was probably the reason, but surely musical curiosity too. When he gave no title to important collections of music (the *Orgelbüchlein* originally, the Eighteen Chorales, the *Well-Tempered Clavier* Book II, the B minor Mass, the *Art of Fugue*) was it modesty or procrastination? When he chose the anonymous-sounding title 'Keyboard Practice' ('Clavierübung') for four quite extraordinary collections of music, was he avoiding the day's many fanciful titles, including his own 'Well-Tempered Clavier' and 'Upright

Instruction'?[1] Or, since 'Keyboard Practice' was a phrase coined by his predecessor Kuhnau, was the allusion as complex as allusions often are – partly modest, partly pretend-modest, saluting a predecessor and his legacy, superseding and improving on it, and so aiming for a significance beyond the usual ephemera?

In the case of Bach's aims, taste, preferences, interests, energy and single-mindedness as a composer, one can give similarly varied answers. If in the course of a work he introduces the theme upside down, is he 'tirelessly exploring the full potential of his thematic ideas', or is he being over-thorough, pedantic, mistaking the intellectual for the artistic, allowing craft to replace art? Either may be the case, especially if his work is compared with that of his gifted contemporaries Handel and Scarlatti, and would say something about him as a composer and as a person.

Arguing from the music to the person, biographers of the last two centuries or so have brought forward many hypotheses about the devices and desires of J. S. Bach, doing so according to fashions in biography. A certain little canon 'reflects a metaphysical dimension to his musical thought'; a certain cantata chorus follows the divine proportion; the fondness for death-texts reveals an orphan's inescapable subconscious. Although the verb in such hypotheses is often vague (what it is that musical sound actually *does*), various such avenues are explored by enthusiasts. Thus the *Musical Offering* explicitly conveys the guidelines of the Latin rhetorician Quintilian; or it does no such thing, but rather 'promotes a biblical understanding of regal glory' with respect to 'Luther's theology of the cross'. Certain words in the text of 'Phoebus and Pan' (BWV 201) are a political joke, a sarcastic allusion to current politicians and Leipzig's municipal factions. Solo concertos evoke the Enlightenment period's cult of the individual, the one against many. In 'Wachet auf!', the composer 'employs his musical techniques to mirror a viable world order', including (in the duets) the masterful

---

[1] The latter, 'Auffrichtige Anleitung', was the fair-copy title for sets of pieces called variously by him 'Praeambulum', 'Fantasia', 'Inventio' and 'Sinfonia', i.e. the two- and three-part Inventions.

male dominating the submissive female. Any time fourteen anythings can be counted there is a self-reference, as of course with any B A C H motif, even when transposed (but is not a 'transposed B A C H' a contradiction in terms?). A conventional emblem such as a rising line or the up-down-up shape of the so-called cross motif always signifies something specific, even when the music is instrumental, without words or any allusion to them. And so on.

One hypothesis about Bach concerns his feelings for his first son Wilhelm Friedemann, born in 1710. Clues from the worklist that they were particularly close are only circumstantial but cannot be matched with the biographies of other sons, and they concern important works:

Clavierbüchlein (1720)
> Instruction book compiled for Friedemann, begun when he was nine years old; evidently rebound in Halle after 1750 (at Friedemann's instigation?). Sources hint at a yet earlier notebook.

The Inventions and the *Well-Tempered Clavier* Book I (1722)
> For Friedemann's next phase of study?

Orgelbüchlein (1723?), a new title for an older set of chorales
> For Friedemann's particular use? A rubric to BWV 605 in the autograph MS is overwritten by the young Friedemann (BJ 2001, p. 67), suggesting he used the book.

Six sonatas for organ, compiled and fair-copied c1729
> Said by Forkel 1802 to have been for Friedemann, who had probably told him so.

Six partitas for harpsichord, published 1731 as a set
> Nos. 3 and 6 for Anna Magdalena? Nos. 1, 2, 4 and 5 (composed subsequently) for Friedemann?

Praeludium in G major for organ, recopied c1733
> For Friedemann's successful audition at the Sophienkirche, Dresden. (Perhaps a different piece had been fair-copied for his unsuccessful application at Halle in March 1731?)

Clavierübung II, published 1735
> Friedemann, now in Dresden, would have found two-manual harpsichords more *au courant*, hence the specification of the title page? (Extant examples by the Gräbner family date from 1722 and 1739.)

Four Lutheran masses, BWV 233–236, late 1730s
For Friedemann in the Sophienkirche, Dresden? Or in connection with possible promotion to the Frauenkirche?
Contrapuntal exercises in the hand of J. S. and W. F. Bach, probably from 1736/8 (Wollny 2002b, p. 278)
A musical 'conversation' between colleagues who drafted canons, fugues and invertible counterpoint in stile antico. (The Art of Fugue subject-head appears here.) The MS supports Emanuel's description of his father starting off fugue study in two parts.[2] MS perhaps from when J. S. was in Dresden (1736) or W. F. in Leipzig (1738).

Harpsichord concertos BWV 1052–1057 as a set, c1738
For Friedemann's concerts in Dresden, or on various (undocumented) returns to Leipzig?
Clavierübung III, published 1739
For Friedemann as a professional organist in Dresden, planning recitals?
Goldberg Variations, published 1741
For Friedemann, virtuoso harpsichordist in Dresden, to play in private concerts? (The dedication of Friedemann's Sonata Fk 5, 1763, to J. G. Goldberg's patron Count von Keyserlingk, suggests a continuing connection between them.)
Copy by J. S. of Friedemann's Concerto for two harpsichords Fk 10
The only known complete copy by J. S. of a work by any son. For performance together?
Cantata 34, c1746
Possibly prepared by the composer for Friedemann's first Whit Sunday in the Liebfrauenkirche, Halle.
Bach's visit to the court in Potsdam, May 1747
Accompanied by Friedemann (who was looking for a position?).
Schübler Chorales, published c1748
Transcribed for (perhaps by) Friedemann? Sold by him in Halle.

Although many of these works had other purposes, the question is still whether they originally had any special connection with Friedemann. It

[2] This much-quoted reference to Bach's teaching methods (Dok III, p. 289) says less than it appears to. For how could one begin study of fugue except by composing a second part? Is Emanuel implying that such ways of studying fugue as today's passive analysis were certainly not his father's?

would be especially helpful to know how common it was for Friedemann to return to Leipzig, bringing distinguished Dresden musicians with him (one documented visit, August 1739), and whose idea it was that he should use some of his father's cantatas in Halle (BWV 31, 34, 50). A clearer sign, perhaps, is the sheer technical difficulty of Friedemann's harpsichord music of the 1730s and 40s, surely derived from or prompted by the six partitas, which were all-too-convincingly described by one early player of them as 'making me seem like a beginner each time' (*Dok* II, p. 223). Did the father encourage the son to apply for the Leipzig cantorate when the church was being pressured to find a successor in 1749, helping him prepare an audition cantata? He could have encouraged Emanuel equally, however, and it was he and not Friedemann who did apply in 1750. The documentation is altogether too ambiguous on incidents that might be very significant. Was Friedemann's absence without leave from Halle for several months after his father's death (*Dok* II, p. 513) purely to oversee the probate process and organise the family in Leipzig, or was he too affected by bereavement even to request formally a leave of absence?

Both sons told anecdotes of their father's musical intimacy with them, of a kind familiar in many a musical family: Emanuel, about being nudged by him when he could predict what was to happen in a fugue they were listening to together (*Dok* III, p. 285);[3] Friedemann, that he joked with him about going to hear the 'nice little Dresden songs' in the court opera (Forkel 1802, p. 49). How well either son mastered the musical demands placed on him is doubtful: a twelve-year-old will not easily conquer Book I of the *Well-Tempered Clavier*. But when c1730–3 Friedemann taught keyboard privately to C. Nichelmann, a chorister at St Thomas's, it was presumably something set up by his father, who taught Nichelmann in class (*Dok* III, p. 106).

Evidence for any special relationship between Sebastian and Friedemann comes only through a few documented contacts, a shared

---

[3] A less picturesque reference to this ability had already been made in the Obituary (*Dok* III, p. 87).

desire to be successful in Dresden (several visits together already in the late 1720s?), the signs of a common enthusiasm for keyboard and contrapuntal music. Without Forkel's note that the six sonatas for organ were written for Friedemann, one could only guess that they were, based on their sources (a copy made by Friedemann) and their chronology (Friedemann was at an appropriate age, nineteen to twenty). Taking such speculaton further, one could hazard a guess that other compositions had Friedemann at least partly in mind: for example, the six sonatas for violin and harpsichord (compiled about the time of his violin study with J. G. Graun in Merseburg, c1726),[4] the Sonata for violin and continuo BWV 1021 (copy part autograph, part Anna Magdalena's hand), and even the first two movements of the B minor Mass, dedicated to the new elector a month or so after Friedemann moved to his capital city.

Friedemann's special efforts with his first cantata in Halle in 1746 recall his father's at Leipzig in 1723, the two being of similar age at similar career points. And if it is possible that the late revised collection of chorale settings, the so-called Eighteen Chorales, was made (in part) to help forward Friedemann's career as a well-known organist, so might the Schübler Chorale transcriptions have been. Friedemann seems to have owned both early and late autographs of his father's organ works, including one of the earliest extant examples (the earliest?) of his handwriting. Did he once possess a second, revised autograph of Book II of the *Well-Tempered Clavier*, now missing (he certainly knew the extant autograph copy)? Any later selling off of his father's manuscripts, even claiming at least one of them as his own work (the organ concerto BWV 596), need not imply any disrespect: there are many reasons for disposing of a heritage, including anguish.

It is tempting to find in all this an explanation for Friedemann's relative failure in life after 1750, despite the King of Prussia's high opinion of him and Emanuel's view that 'he could replace our father

---

[4] Graun was later concertmeister to Frederick II in Potsdam, while Friedemann's pupil Nichelmann was second harpsichordist. Was this another reason for Friedemann to accompany his father on the visit of 1747?

better than the rest of us together' (Dok III, pp. 276, 613). In much the same way, one can speculate that their younger brother Gottfried Bernhard's problems – debts as a young organist, leaving a good job precipitously, moving to another city where another Bach lived (Johann Nikolaus Bach, in Jena) – arose in part from avoiding Leipzig, or his stepmother, or his awesome father?

For Friedemann, the case may be a little clearer. Had he been over-encouraged – outwardly or inwardly – by a driven and driving father, overburdened by living up to expectations, over-dependent on him, and over-afflicted by his death? He saw his younger brother become more obviously successful, even as an author writing about the field (keyboard playing) in which he, Friedemann, was regarded by many as the true apostolic successor. There are many if inconclusive hints that father and son remained close for forty years. Was it a case of special love for a first son, recognition of an unusual talent, a keen desire to discern one? Anxiety to compensate for the early loss of his mother, doubt that he was robust or had the stamina or killer instinct required for great success? Inadvertent domination, making such success impossible?

APPENDIX 2: SOME TERMS

Affekt: the mood of a piece of music or the feelings aroused in its listener, particularly as invoked by such details as style, key and *figurae* (q.v.).

Brustwerk: the small organ chest (usually played by its own manual) above the keyboards 'in the breast' of the organ, often used for continuo (q.v.).

cantor: in Lutheran Germany, the musician in charge of a church's music, who also taught in its school and directed music on public municipal occasions.

capellmeister: musician in charge of a court's *cappella* (q.v.), its personnel and its performances, both sacred (cantatas in chapel, etc.) and secular (chamber music, opera, etc.).

cappella: the company of singers and instrumentalists performing a range of musical duties for their employer (church, court).

chair organ: the little organ behind the organist's back, usually in the gallery front, played by the lowest keyboard.

Clavier: 'keyboard' instrument, of whatever kind was appropriate or conventional in the circumstances.

concertmeister: c1715, a recent term for the leading instrumentalist (first violinist or continuo player?) organising, rehearsing and conducting the band.

concerto grosso: an ensemble ('consort') which, in Italian usage, contains a small group of soloists contrasting with the tutti; a piece of music for this ensemble.

consort: old English term for an ensemble of instruments, either of one family (e.g. 'viol consort') or of mixed strings and wind ('broken consort').

continuo: simple accompaniment created by the keyboardist playing the bass line and the chords that it implies or that its figures indicate.

cross motif: four notes whose first and last are of much the same pitch, the second higher and the third lower (or vice versa), so that the two lines connecting 1 with 4 and 2 with 3 form a cross.

elector: one of the nine German princes entitled, by 1693, to elect the (Holy Roman) Emperor. In this book, 'king' and 'queen' are sometimes used for the Elector and Electress of Saxony, since the elector was also King of Poland.

figura: a 'figure' or distinctive note pattern in a particular shape, catalogued by such contemporary theorists as J. G. Walther.

galant: eighteenth-century term now applied to light, elegant music of the period, mostly not for church.

'Germany': the Peace of Westphalia (1648) gave the individual dukedoms, kingdoms, etc. of German-speaking Europe the power to form their own alliances, making them practically independent states. The formal (though hardly cultural) unity of 'one Germany' was achieved only in 1871.

Hanseatic: referring to a city, usually important, with strong municipal institutions and belonging to the Hanse, a German commercial league; see maps.

ordre: a French keyboard suite of dances, an 'order' (category group) in the same class, e.g. a certain tonic, major and/or minor.

organ chorale: a setting or reworking of a Lutheran hymn melody for organ, often called 'chorale prelude' but not necessarily a prelude to anything, and with few exceptions longer and more intricate than a verse of the hymn.

ostinato: an 'obstinate' phrase which recurs throughout a piece of music.

praeludium: specifically, a major 'prelude' for organ, in several sections or movements, thus corresponding to early instrumental sonatas.

privilege: the right exercised by a craftsman such as an organ builder to accept as many contracts in a specified territory as he wishes.

reeds: organ pipes with a reed (like a clarinet), creating power and variety. A 32′ reed is a rare, loud stop sounding two octaves below the written note.

rubato: a later term denoting flexibility of the beat, used for expressive purposes.

stoplist: the contracted-for number and types of stops in a given organ, the more the bigger and more important the instrument.

suboctave: the sound an 'octave below' notated pitch, given by certain sets of harpsichord strings or organ pipes.

vespers: for Lutherans, an afternoon or evening service with NT canticles, shorter and lighter than the 'Main Service' but often with important music, including organ solos and special choral items: something of a 'church concert'.

REFERENCES

Adlung, Jakob, 1768. *Musica mechanica organoedi*, ed. Johann Lorenz
Albrecht, Berlin.

Andreas Bach Book = Leipziger Städtische Bibliotheken,
Musikbibliothek, MS III.8.4.

Bach, Carl Philipp Emanuel, 1753, 1762. *Versuch über die wahre Art das
Clavier zu spielen*, 2 vols., Berlin.

BJ = *Bach-Jahrbuch*.

Burney, Charles, 1789. *A General History of Music*, vol. IV, London.

Camerarius, Joachimus, 1566. *De Philippi Melanchthonis ortu*, Leipzig.

Cox, Howard H. (ed.), 1985. *The Calov Bible of J. S. Bach*, Ann Arbor, MI.

Dähnert, Ulrich, 1962. *Der Orgel- und Instrumentenbauer Zacharias
Hildebrandt*, Leipzig.

Dok I, II, III = *Bach-Dokumente*, vol. I, ed. Werner Neumann and
Hans-Joachim Schulze, Kassel, 1963; vol. II, ed. Werner
Neumann and Hans-Joachim Schulze, Kassel, 1969; vol. III, ed.
Hans-Joachim Schulze, Kassel, 1972.

DTÖ = *Denkmäler der Tonkunst in Österreich*.

Forkel, Johann Nicolaus, 1802. *Ueber Johann Sebastian Bachs Leben, Kunst
und Kunstwerke*, Leipzig.

Gallico, Claudio, 1986. *Girolamo Frescobaldi. L'affetto, l'ordito, le
metamorfosi*, Florence.

Geiringer, Karl, 1954. *The Bach Family*, London.

Glöckner, Andreas, 1988. 'Gründe für Johann Sebastian Bachs
    Weggang von Weimar', in Winfried Hoffmann and Armin
    Schneiderheinze (eds.), *Bericht über die wissenschaftliche Konferenz
    zum V. Internationalen Bachfest der DDR 1985*, Leipzig, pp. 137–43.

2002. '"Na, die hätten Sie aber auch nur hören sollen!" Über die
    Unzulänglichkeiten bei Bachs Leipziger Figuralaufführungen',
    in Ulrich Leisinger (ed.), *Bach in Leipzig – Bach und Leipzig*.
    Konferenzbericht Leipzig 2000, Hildesheim, pp. 387–401.

Heinichen, Johann David, 1711. *Neu erfundene und gründliche Anweisung
    zu vollkommener Erlernung des General-Basses*, Hamburg.

HHB = Bernd Baselt et al. (eds.), *Händel-Handbuch Band 4: Dokumente zu
    Leben und Schaffen*, Kassel and Leipzig, 1984.

Hübner, Johann, 1717–37. *Genealogische Tabellen*, 4 vols., Leipzig.

Küster, Konrad, 1996. *Der junge Bach*, Stuttgart.

[Mainwaring, John,] 1760. *Memoirs of the Life of the Late George Frederic
    Handel*, London.

Marshall, Robert L., 2000. 'Toward a Twenty-First-Century Bach
    Biogaphy', *Musical Quarterly* 84 (Fall), pp. 497–525.

Mattheson, Johannes, 1722, 1725. *Critica musica*, 2 vols., Hamburg.

    1731. *Grosse General-Bass-Schule, oder: der exemplarischen Organisten-Probe
    zweite, verbesserte und vermehrte Auflage*, Hamburg.

    1739. *Der vollkommene Capellmeister*, Hamburg.

    1740. *Grundlage einer Ehren-Pforte*, Hamburg.

Möller MS = Staatsbibliothek zu Berlin, Preussischer Kulturbesitz,
    Musikabteilung, MS 40644.

NBA, KB = *Neue Bach-Ausgabe, Kritischer Bericht* [Critical Commentary].

NBR = Hans T. David and Arthur Mendel (eds.), *The New Bach Reader*,
    revised and enlarged by Christoph Wolff, New York, 1998.

Niedt, Friedrich Erhard, 1721. *Musicalische Handleitung*, part II edited
    and enlarged by Johann Mattheson, Hamburg.

Obituary = Dok III, pp. 80–93.

Palisca, Claude V., 1994. *Studies in the History of Italian Music and Music
    Theory*, Oxford.

Petzoldt, Martin, 2000. *Bachstätten. Ein Reiseführer zu Johann Sebastian Bach*, Frankfurt am Main.

Pirro, André, 1907. *L'esthétique de J. S. Bach*, Paris.

Quantz, Johann Joachim, 1752. *Versuch einer Anweisung die Flöte traversiere zu spielen*, Berlin.

Rameau, Jean-Philippe, 1722. *Traité de l'harmonie reduite à ses principes naturels*, Paris.

1726. *Nouveau système de musique théorique*, Paris.

Schneider, Wolfgang, 1995. *Leipzig. Streifzüge durch die Kulturgeschichte*, 2nd edn, Leipzig.

Spitta, Philipp, 1873, 1880. *Johann Sebastian Bach*, 2 vols., Leipzig.

Szeskus, Reinhard, 1991. *Johann Sebastian Bachs historischer Ort* = Bach-Studien 10, Leipzig.

Titon Du Tillet, Evard, 1732. *Le Parnasse françois*, Paris.

Walther, Johann Gottfried, 1732. *Musicalisches Lexicon*, Leipzig.

1955. *Praecepta der musicalischen Composition* [1708], ed. Peter Benary, Leipzig.

Werckmeister, Andreas, 1698. *Erweiterte und verbesserte Orgelprobe*, 2nd enlarged edn, Quedlinburg.

Wolff, Christoph, 2000. *Johann Sebastian Bach: The Learned Musician*, Oxford.

Wollny, Peter, 2002a. 'On Miscellaneous American Bach Sources', *Bach Perspectives* 5, pp. 131–50.

2002b. 'Ein Quellenfund in Kiew. Unbekannte Kontrapunktstudien von Johann Sebastian und Wilhelm Friedemann Bach', in Ulrich Leisinger (ed.), *Bach in Leipzig – Bach und Leipzig. Konferenzbericht Leipzig 2000*, Hildesheim, pp. 275–87.

BWV INDEX

The text may refer to a work by title rather than BWV number

INDEX OF NAMES